1991

504

D0390636

"A real why-you-should and how-you-can book. Saturated with pearls of wisdom and common-sense advice that will take you from where you are to where you want to go. I learned from it and so will you."
Zig Ziglar

"Throughout this book Dexter Yager shares the most important secrets of life: That failure is the essential ingredient in building personal character to sustain us through success, and that the source of all power comes from God."
John McCormack

Everything I Know at the Top
I Learned at the Bottom

Dexter Yager
and
Ron Ball

Tyndale House Publishers, Inc.
Wheaton, Illinois

Library of Congress Catalog Card Number 91-75018
ISBN 0-8423-4903-0
Copyright © 1991 by Dexter Yager and Ron Ball
All rights reserved
Printed in the United States of America

96	95	94	93	92	91	
7	6	5	4	3	2	1

ACKNOWLEDGMENTS

To Ron Ball, once again, for his willingness and patience to spend countless hours and endless nights working with me on this book. His effort, through lengthy interviews and phone calls, to organize my thoughts on paper in a clear, understandable way was far from an easy task.

To my father, Leonard E. Yager, Sr., who, although no longer with us, has been my guiding light and strong example, not only when I was a child, but throughout my adult years as well. I have always been appreciative especially of those life lessons I learned from him. They have never been more real to me than during his last days, the past few months—he passed away just one month ago, during the completion of this manuscript.

To my mother, Gertrude, who continues to carry his torch. In many ways she filled the gaps and gave me what he could not. She is a continual source of inspiration to me.

To my wife, Birdie, who has been loyal and committed to me and my dreams for thirty-four years.

To my brother, Richard "Butch" Yager, whom I respect greatly. I very much appreciate his loyalty and service in business as well as in the tradition of family. He is one of my very best friends!

And to my seven children, who with their mates are each finding, in their own way and pace, the lessons of leadership from the bottom up. DEXTER YAGER

It has been a joy to work again with Dexter Yager. He is truly a great man who is an unfailing delight and inspiration. My thanks also to Ken Petersen, a talented and committed editor. His attitude and competence make him a pleasure. Cliff Johnson and his staff have again been invaluable. They are an effective, productive team. Sincere thanks to my greatest teachers, my wife Amy and my daughter Allison. They motivate me to be a better man. Thank you God for them! And thanks to Mom and Dad who taught me to dream. RON BALL

CONTENTS

Introduction	You Start at the Bottom	*1*
One	Decide What Your Dream Is	*9*
Two	Make a Plan	*21*
Three	Overcome Dream Deflators	*31*
Four	Build on the Right Foundation	*47*
Five	Keep Your Momentum	*61*
Six	Develop Big-League Thinking	*73*
Seven	Make Yourself Worthy	*91*
Eight	Prevent Your Dream from Getting the Best of You	*103*
Nine	Sometimes You Have to Fight	*123*
Ten	Discover the Special Ingredient	*137*

Introduction
You Start at the Bottom

Your success and happiness lie in you. External conditions are the accidents of life.

HELEN KELLER

It's interesting to me how many people think that success is a matter of getting lucky. A man gambles half his week's salary on a ball game for a shot at a windfall. A woman plays the lottery for a chance at $20 million and a way to leapfrog out of middle-class mediocrity into success and wealth. Siblings contest the will of a deceased mother or father for a shot at a bigger share of the estate and a ticket to prosperity.

People think success is something that's given to them.

I happen to own ten corporations, some thirty or so real estate holdings and buildings, several beautiful homes, and lots of cars. One definition of a millionaire is someone who doesn't know all that he owns. Truth is, I lost count a long time ago. It's a fact—I'm a multimillionaire.

People often ask me how I got to be so lucky. And the thing is, I don't know how to answer a question like that.

On the one hand, I'll be the first to admit I'm fortunate. I know other people are less fortunate, and I'm grateful for what God has given me.

On the other hand, I don't consider myself lucky because, quite honestly, I earned it.

My success wasn't won by playing Lotto, and it wasn't given to me through an inheritance. My success was achieved through hard work, risk taking, and a dream that I had a long time ago and have cultivated through the years.

And most of all, my success has been a lifelong process of learning. Learning from others, learning from my failures, learning by doing.

Everything I know at the top, I learned at the bottom.

People are always looking for the secret to success. There are lots of A-B-C and 1-2-3 books on the bookshelves. Experts share their formulas for making money and getting rich. CEOs write about their experiences and how they made it to the top.

Maybe it will surprise you to hear me say this, but I believe the secret to success is that *there are no secrets to success*. The formula for wealth is that *there is no formula*. If you think this book is going to tell you some secret or share with you some formula, I'll tell you now that it won't, and I'll advise you to put it back on the table or bookshelf where you found it.

I have written a number of books on the subjects of success and wealth. Each book is the same in this way: I don't claim to give you a secret or a formula. I simply wish to share with you my experiences in hopes that they may help you in some way. I include in many of my books tips and pieces of advice that might be useful to you. But, frankly, they're not secrets, and they're not guaranteed formulas or recipes. They're just the basic ingredients. You have to put them in the bowl of your life and stir.

My success has been a lifelong process of learning. Learning from others, learning from my failures, learning by doing.

Someone once said, "An education is something a person gets for himself, not that which someone else gives or does to him." Learning the principles of success depends on you—not on me, and not on this book.

You need to pursue the basic principles of success while you're at the bottom in order to know anything about success at the top.

The simple truth is that success is something you dream of and then something you work for.

One of the first lessons I learned at the bottom was when I was at the *very* bottom: I was just a kid. Let's just say I was still working toward my first million!

I decided then, when I was in sixth grade, that I was going to pursue my dream of having my own business.

Growing up, I always wanted my own business. I don't know why, although my family had something to do with that. My mother would always say, "Yagers just don't work for someone else. They've gotta be their own boss." I somehow had that instinct in me, and I felt it strongly: I needed to be in charge of my own dream.

So I decided then, when I was in sixth grade, that I was going to pursue my dream of having my own business.

I made myself a distributor—a middleman—although I wouldn't have understood those terms at the time. I bought soda pop for a nickel a bottle and then sold it to construction workers on the job for a dime a bottle. I was a distributor, bringing refreshments to people who had a need for them but no access to them. I used ice from our refrigerator at home. Soon my little business was a big success.

A little too big perhaps. I was soon selling whole cases of soda pop, and I was making some pretty good money. Others noticed. Some adults copied my idea and started delivering ice and drinks as well. I suddenly had competition.

This was my first lesson. It has since become a favorite phrase of mine and the title of one of my first books: "Don't let anybody steal your dream."

I could have let my dream be stolen. I was just a kid. Nobody expected me to make as much as I had made; nobody expected me to compete with adult competition. But I had that certain something in me, that Yager mind-set perhaps, and I decided to fight for my dream. I hired other kids to help me. We diversified our selection of drinks and made sure we never ran out of ice. And, believe it or not, we eventually beat out our competition. It was too much work for them. We earned our permanent place in that market.

I was just a kid, but I learned an adult lesson: If you have a dream, pursue it. Don't let it go, and don't give it up without a fight. I was at the very bottom of my fledgling career as an businessman and entrepreneur, but I learned a principle that I use nearly every day of my adult life. Everything I know at the top, I learned at the bottom.

Success isn't a matter of getting lucky. Do you know that a lot of past lottery winners are penniless today? They were given wealth, but they never developed the knowledge to use it wisely. They got "to the top" without having learned anything at the bottom. Their so-called success wasn't built on any foundation of knowledge and experience. Eventually they squandered their windfall.

You can learn lessons now that will be the key to your getting to the top and staying there. Most of what you learn will be through your own experiences of pursuing your dream, succeeding, and, yes, sometimes failing. But maybe some of the lessons I've learned in my life, some of the basic ingredients of success that I can share with you in this book, will assist you as well.

I hope what I know at the top might help you get there too.

One
Decide What Your Dream Is

If one advances confidently in the direction of his dreams, and endeavors to live the life which he has imagined, he will meet with a success unexpected in common hours.

HENRY DAVID THOREAU

Early in my adult life I worked in an auto dealership. That's right—I used to be a car salesman. Now, car salesmen aren't very high on anyone's prestige list. To me it was a serious job, and I learned a lot that has come in handy later in life. But many people look down on car salesmen and treat them rudely. Someone once said that a good salesman is someone who has found a cure for the common cold shoulder.

People were rude to me too, but, although I never really found the antidote for the common cold shoulder, I tried to rise above the condescending attitudes and concentrate instead on what I knew I could become eventually, later in life. I reminded myself that selling cars was a temporary job, that eventually I would ascend to greater heights, but that for now I had to be the very best salesman I could possibly be.

During this time I had a secret dream. That dream was to own an expensive car. This dream of mine carried me through many a sales pitch and helped me remain confident and positive even when the people I was dealing with were rude and nasty. The lesson I learned then was simple: I realized the power of having a dream.

My dream accomplished many things for me, and it gave me the motivation to persevere. Not only that, but eventually it came true. I eventually bought that expensive car. And another. And another. Today I have a seventeen-car garage that houses two Rolls Royces and a number of other cars, which I collect for my personal enjoyment.

I hope you don't misunderstand me. It's not the cars or the wealth that matters. It's not what you have that counts, but rather the power of your dream. The lesson I learned when I was at the bottom was that I needed a dream.

You're no different. You need a dream to drive you to great heights of achievement in your life.

Recently a company held a seminar and invited some teenagers to participate. One of the workshops was a discussion session, and one young man spoke with remarkable honesty. He told how growing up he had watched the adults around him, and many of them were people who had abandoned their goals and desires. They had suffered disappointments and difficulties and just quit working toward their dreams. This young man said, "You know, I've thought a lot about these grown-ups and how they just quit on their dreams. I don't think we should call them grown-ups any more. I think we ought to call them 'given-ups,' because that's all they do."

You know a lot of given-ups. You've met them, you work with them, maybe you're related to them. Their whole approach to life is survival—how they can hang on long enough until they can make it to the next paycheck.

Having a dream transports you out of the frustrations of the present into the possibilities of the future.

I want you to know you are better than that. God intended you to live beyond mediocrity.

A man I know of, Bill O'Brian works for Hanover Insurance. He once spoke about the young men and women who start with his corporation and what happens to them. He said, "People enter business as bright, high-energy people. They are full of desire to make a difference. By the time they are thirty, a few of them are fast trackers, but the rest put in their time and do what matters to them on the weekend. They lose the commitment, the sense of mission, and the excitement with which they started. We get little of their energy and almost none of their spirit."

These are given-ups. They start with great vision, wonderful hopes, and powerful dreams. Then they experience a reversal, some rejections, personal criticisms, and they decide to join the growing population of given-ups. What a terrible way to live. As one author puts it: "It's like being in a race to get first where nobody even wants to go."

Today people wake up when they're in their thirties, and realize that they're not who they really wanted to be.

One research study from the Massachusetts Institute of Technology determined that when people are asked what they want out of life, the majority of people answer negatively. They talk about how terrible their job is or all the things they wish were different. They don't have a positive goal. They don't have a positive dream that pulls them to greater, higher levels of achievement and accomplishment. They tell you what they want to get rid of. "I don't want my mother-in-law to live with me anymore." "I want to get rid of this rattletrap of a car that I ride around in." "I want to get out of this small, cramped house." "I want to feel better." "I want to lose all of this weight."

Can you imagine living your whole life where

your reward is built on making it to Friday night? Where your goal is partying on the weekend? Where your greatest accomplishment each week is surviving your job? Maybe you can imagine these things. Maybe you don't have a dream.

In my book *The Mark of a Millionaire* I wrote about the "basics of dreaming." I said there were three things that having a dream does for you.

First, *a dream gives you a future focus.* Instead of being preoccupied with the frustrations of the present, a dream gets you thinking about the possibilities of the future. I've often told the story of the time I was driving around the Lake Wylie, South Carolina, area. I pulled off to the side of an undeveloped property. There was a bulldozer on the land. Some trees were down. There was a lot of mud. Frankly, it looked awful. It was ugly and unappealing.

But it occurred to me that even though it looked ugly to me, there was somebody somewhere who would say it was beautiful. Because to someone that property represents a dream. The way that dreamer sees it, the property looks the way he will *make it look* with his ideas and sweat and creativity. He might go there every day to delight in his dream. He might see a vision of the home he's going to build on that property. It's the focus of his future. Many times the dreams of your life are

15

right around you. It's a matter of what you make of it.

A dream gives you energy. The problem with so many of the given-ups of this world is that they have no energy. If they had a dream to work toward they'd simply get a lot more done in life.

You have to have energy—something flowing through you—to give you the power to get up in the morning. I had a stroke in 1986, and there was a great deal of physical pain during my recuperation. Sometimes I didn't want to get up in the morning. But then suddenly I'd begin to think about my dreams, my goals, what I wanted for the network, and the thousands of people who depended on me. Soon I wasn't in bed anymore.

The problem with so many of the given-ups of this world is that they have no energy. If they had a dreamthey'd simply get a lot more done in life.

A dream keeps you from wasting your life. Today people wake up when they're in their thirties, and realize that they're not who they really wanted to be. Their life doesn't have anything to show for their years. They panic, suddenly regretting the way they've wasted time. They wonder why they didn't accomplish more. They find themselves in mid-life crisis. They wish they had chosen differently—a different school or career or spouse. But their real problem isn't making better choices—it has to do with their failure to pursue a dream.

I knew a man who had accomplished some things in life but never reached his potential. He was in his sixties. We were talking, and he was recalling parts of his life and expressing his dissatisfaction with himself. I asked him why he was disappointed in his life. He said, "Because I never learned to dream dreams. My dreams were there at one time, and I just kind of let them go."

So many people today are facing a mid-life crisis because they never learned to dream dreams. Their lives are sequences of events that happened to them rather than stories of dreams dreamed, pursued, and fulfilled.

When people have dreams and nurture and develop them, they become successful.

Your dreams protect you against wasting your life. I'm talking about the waste of yourself—your talents, abilities, and your creativity. You don't have to go through a mid-life crisis. If you have dreams, and if you believe your dreams can come true, you will wake up at fifty or sixty and realize not only how much you've accomplished but how much you really still want to accomplish. Regret will never enter your mind—you won't have time for that because you'll be planning your next dream!

You need to dream because you need something to pull you toward achievement. You need something to get you through all the muck and mire that threatens to suck you down and hold you back. You need something to give you the energy to move forward. You know already that many people don't have great dreams, and many people abandon their dreams early in life. You look at schoolchildren, and they're full of excitement and enthusiasm, but as they grow up they begin to feel the hard knocks of life. Everything collapses. They get their teeth knocked out, their stomach kicked in, and suddenly they begin to think, "Maybe I shouldn't go for great things. Maybe I shouldn't try to dream." They become given-ups instead of grown-ups.

When people don't pursue a dream, a little part of them dies inside. When people have dreams and nurture and develop them, they become successful. It's that simple.

So you need a dream. It is what can save you from meaninglessness. It is what can give you a happy, fulfilled life.

You don't want to be a given-up. You don't want to be thirty or forty or fifty and barely surviving with no energy left in you. You don't want to be someone who is just surviving a job to make it to the next weekend or the next vacation. You don't want to live your whole life with goals that are negatives you want to escape from.

You need a dream, a dream that will take your breath away.

Two
Make a Plan

A goal is a dream with a deadline.

ANONYMOUS

When I was building my first business, I lived in Rome, New York. I had business associates in North Carolina, and I regularly had to travel back and forth between both places of business.

I had been making a plan to help my business grow. I needed a southern city for the plan, a place with a warm climate, an area just beginning a growth cycle in real estate. Part of my plan was to settle in a respected part of this city, an address that would command respect and credibility.

One time as I was driving from New York to North Carolina, I found myself passing through the city of Charlotte, and it flashed into my head that this was the perfect city I had been looking for in my business plan. My wife, Birdie, and I settled there. We found the best section of town and located our first Charlotte home there.

Not long after the move, I was buying furniture. I requested delivery, and was told that my check needed to be cleared first. But as I provided my address, the salesperson stopped and said, "Oh, I didn't realize you lived in that part of town. In this case, we'll be happy to deliver your furniture right away!"

All of this was due to the simple fact that I had developed a plan and had put it into action. My dream was to extend my business in a specific way. I created a detailed plan—right down to the matter of where I'd live. Because I had a plan, when I found the city of my dream, I was able to act quickly, and my dream came true.

You know, it's funny that most people aren't comfortable with dreaming dreams. You'd think it would come naturally. Just imagine yourself in the best situations. Just let your mind go. But most people seem afraid to let themselves dream dreams—or at least to take them seriously.

The problem is that for many people a dream seems impossible to achieve. It's so big and overwhelming that it almost seems ridiculous—"You mean *me*, a millionaire?!" People are afraid to take their dreams seriously because their dreams are larger than anything they've dealt with before in life.

Of course, that's what makes a dream a dream! It should be bigger than life. It should seem impossible to achieve. It should be worth striving for. It should take your breath away.

The secret that many people haven't discovered is the secret of defining their dreams. Most people haven't learned how to break their dreams down into smaller, manageable, achievable units. They haven't learned the art of defining goals.

Let me give you a simple, six-step method of doing this:

1. *Write down your dreams*. Now you may be thinking that this is a little silly. Maybe you think you can keep them in your head well enough. Why do you need to write them down? Let me tell you a story:

IBM once conducted an exercise that involved upper- and middle-management executives. IBM sat everyone down in a room. There were about two hundred participants. They were told to take out a piece of paper. "You have two hours," the group was told. "Use your imagination and write down exactly what you're going to be doing on your perfect day five years from today." The group was instructed to make it extremely detailed: What time they would awaken. What toothpaste they would use. What they would eat for breakfast. If they were married and had children and where family members might be during the day. What they, as executives, might be doing at nine and ten and eleven in the morning as well as throughout the afternoon and evening.

IBM found that only 3 percent of the group

had ever done that kind of exercise. Yet by writing down their *perfect day,* most of the executives gained a clear vision of what their dreams really were.

Have you ever done an exercise like that? You need to. Write down your dreams. Be specific.

Writing down your dreams makes them more practical, more immediate, and less abstract. The written list will remind you of goals you had set for yourself that you wouldn't otherwise be able to remember. The act of writing such a list becomes a commitment on your part that takes the dream beyond the pie-in-the-sky stage and puts it right on the table in front of you.

2. Divide each dream into smaller, achievable, immediate goals. Let's take a hypothetical situation. Say your dream is to lose ten pounds. Start by writing that down on a piece of paper. Next, divide that dream into smaller goals. Perhaps that means losing two pounds a week for the next five weeks. So you really have five smaller goals—two pounds each week for five weeks.

You must turn your dreams into goals.

---

3. Create an action plan. This means beside each of your smaller goals you need to write down the way that you will actively achieve your subgoal. In your effort to lose ten pounds, the first week's plan may be to cut out all desserts. For the second week, you may decide to exercise three mornings. (Probably a better way in this case is to create a plan that includes diet and exercise and repeat that same plan five times, each of five weeks.)

An action plan is usually where you attach deadlines to your goals. As someone once said, "A goal is a dream with a deadline." You have to be careful to make sure your deadlines are realistic. Yet you need to push yourself enough so that you are aggressively pursuing your dream. It's hard to find that balance, but you will—with practice.

4. *Identify the kind of man or woman you need to be to accomplish your goal.* Write this down as well. In your dream of losing ten pounds, you might write that you will need to be the kind of person who can control his appetite and the kind who has discipline to exercise several mornings a week. You might write down that you will need to have willpower to turn down the various snacks and desserts offered to you.

5. *Imagine yourself already having reached that goal.* I've written before about the power of visualization: "What exactly is visualization? It's a mental technique. You picture in vivid, clear terms what it is you really want. You create an intense picture of where you're going. You see yourself having accomplished your dream. That picture is constantly in front of you. You

visualize it, you feel it, you touch it, you taste it, you see it, you live it."

6. *Finally, discover the goal behind the goal.* What is your biggest goal right now? Picture it. Now imagine that this week you reached it. It's done—you did it. Now that you have it, what is it doing for you? What result is it producing? When you identify that result, you'll know the goal behind the goal.

Create an intense picture of where you are going.

For example, let's say you live out in the country. You've stated your dream—to become financially independent and wealthy. One of your goals is to have a house in the city. Now you imagine you already have that house in the city. But what has that house in the city already done for you? Why is it important to you? You begin to think that it puts you close to a good school. You can involve your family in great cultural activities in the city. You and your wife can dine out at fine restaurants. Then those things are your real goals. They are what you're really after. Your goal isn't really a house in the city. That's a means to the goal.

The value of discovering the goal behind the goal is that it can clarify your plan. In the example we just explored, since your real goal isn't the house in the city, maybe you can discover another, better way to achieve those other things than actually buying a house downtown. Maybe it makes more sense to rent an apartment there for a couple of years, or to sublet a place for the summer and send your kids to summer school downtown. Ultimately, discovering the goal behind the goal will help you clarify the steps in your plan.

There's a hidden power in creating a plan to achieve your dream. Can you see what that is?

Think of your goals as targets. A bull's eye counts 100 points; it's the ultimate realization of your dream. Around the bull's eye are rings of color that count for 80, 60, 40, and 20 points. You aim for 100, and maybe you'll hit the bull's eye. But even if you don't, you're likely to hit 60 or even 80 points.

Maybe you'll hit the bull's eye. But even if you don't, you'll likely score higher than if you'd never aimed for the target at all.

After Eisenhower won the Republican nomination for President in 1952, a reporter asked Taft about his goals. He said, "My goal was to become President of the United States in 1953." The reporter smirked. "Well, then you didn't exactly make it, did you?" Taft replied, "No, but then again, I did become a senator from Ohio!"

When you create a set of goals to achieve your dream, you're setting yourself up for success. Maybe you'll hit the bull's eye. But even if you don't, you'll likely score higher than if you'd never aimed for the target at all.

You must make a plan to achieve your dreams. Here it is again in a nutshell: Write down your dream. Write down smaller, achievable goals. Create an action plan. Write down the person you need to be to achieve your goals. Imagine—visualize—yourself having achieved the dream. Discover the goals behind the goals to help you clarify your plan.

Three
Overcome Dream Deflators

Success is to be measured not so much by the position one has received in life as the obstacles he has to overcome while trying to succeed.

ANONYMOUS

When you define your dream, a great many things will rush in to burst your bubble. These are dream deflators, and they are destructive behaviors that are part of each one of us, behaviors that we have to fight to overcome. Otherwise these dream deflators will puncture our dreams every time.

The title of this book, *Everything I Know at the Top, I Learned at the Bottom,* can be taken in more than one way. As I have been telling you, a great many things I learned when I was at the bottom of my career. But let me say that some lessons are only learned when you're at the bottom of life.

Some years ago, when I had my stroke, I faced some terribly dark times. In times like that, your achievements, wealth, and success don't mean much. You simply hope for a chance to achieve more. You begin to regret how little time there is to attain your dreams.

The lesson I learned then—at the

bottom—was that there are all kinds of things in life that try to burst the bubble of your dream. These are dream deflators.

I decided not to let my stroke deflate my dream. I couldn't lie around in the hospital. I'm an achiever. I had something the doctors didn't understand and most still don't, and it finally got me out of the hospital. Oh, my arm may not be working the way it's supposed to, and there are little challenges, but I am walking despite the fact that they predicted that I would have to use a wheelchair for the rest of my life.

What helped me recover as well as I have was the power of my dream and the refusal to let my poor health become a dream deflator. I determined to trust God and fight back. I had more dreams to achieve—I still do—and I won't let anything stand in the way.

Now, maybe poor health is a dream deflator for you, but my guess is that there are other much more common dream deflators that are more likely to stand in your way.

Let me warn you about seven serious dream deflators:

1. *The quick-fix mentality.* Your dreams will never come true if you have a quick-fix attitude. This is the attitude that whispers, "Hurry up!" It means that you can't wait, you can't be patient, you don't have time to work hard and pay your dues, and you have to have everything right now.

You've probably heard the phrase "delayed gratification." I believe in delayed gratification. But it's so easy to mouth those words—and it's so much harder to live them. Of course, the Bible teaches the great principle of delayed gratification. God gives you many extraordinary blessings when you come to know Jesus Christ. One of the greatest blessings is the delayed gratification of a very real dimension known as heaven, about which the Bible says: "Eye has not seen, nor ear heard, nor have entered into the heart of man the things which God has prepared for those who love him." So there's this whole dimension of heaven that we're waiting for. Now, we have great blessings here and now as well—the Bible teaches that also. The principle of delayed gratification applies spiritually as well as to your business and to your attitude. You must get rid of your quick-fix mentality.

I believe in delayed gratification. But it's so easy to mouth those words—and it's so much harder to live them.

You watch television. On a single program they'll present three major life crises and resolve them all within thirty minutes, including commercials. We don't have the patience to watch a story that's more like real life, something that takes time and doesn't always have a tidy ending. I heard this called the "*Reader's Digest* approach"—a lot of people don't even read whole books anymore, they just read *Reader's Digest* for the condensed versions. They don't want to take the time and put in the work for the real book. They want everything in life served to them on a platter.

If you want your dreams to work, quick-fix mentality has got to go.

Let me tell you a secret. If you want your dreams to work, the quick-fix mentality has got to go. I have spent more than thirty-five years building my dreams. I own more than forty business entities. Do you realize that, according to National Chamber of Commerce figures, for every ten businesses or companies that are started in this country, within five years half of them will be gone? Only 40 percent of them will make it past ten years, and only 30 percent of them will make it past fifteen. Do you realize that of the Fortune 500 companies that existed in 1970—the 500 largest, most stable corporations in America—100 of them were out of business by 1983? If that's true corporately, how does that fit your life?

Do you have the long-range vision to stick to your dream? If you have a quick-fix mentality, then you don't. If your goal is to become wealthy, don't think it's going to happen overnight. If you're trying to become a great businessman, don't aim to achieve success in a few months or a year. If you're trying to become a great father and husband, don't think that a few days of changed behavior will turn around years of neglecting your wife and children. The quick-fix mentality just won't cut it.

Look at your budget, examine your bank book, take a hard look at how you live your life and how you spend your money. Then look yourself in the face and tell yourself whether you believe in delayed gratification or not.

Are you willing to shut down your need for immediate gratification in order to wait for your dream to come true?

I heard a man recite this quote about Christian beliefs. "What we believe now as Christians, the early Christians didn't just believe it—they knew it, deep in their heart." That's a quote from Henry Ford, the famous car manufacturer. The great spiritual truth—*they knew*. Many of you believe in the principle of delayed gratification, but do you really know it?

Do you really live it? Are you willing to shut down your need for immediate gratification in order to wait for your dream to come true?

2. The trap of people pleasing. Not everyone will be excited about your dream. Some people may criticize you for striving for something they don't agree with. Others will feel threatened because you're going somewhere with your life, and they're not. But if you let these naysayers inside your head, you'll never achieve success. You'll never attain your dream.

As Herbert Swope once said, "I cannot give you the formula for success, but I can give you the formula for failure—which is: Try to please everybody." Think about people you know who are living at a level of mediocrity. Consider the type of people they are. Isn't it true that many of them are people pleasers? They're always striving to make everyone around them happy, never able to make decisions that might leave someone displeased.

Some people won't like your dream. That's OK. It's your dream, not theirs.

Avoid the trap of people pleasing. Some people won't like your dream. That's OK. It's your dream, not theirs.

3. The manipulation of truth. I mean this in

two ways. First, stop manipulating the truth with other people. Of course, you would never openly lie because you wouldn't want to get caught. But you'll take bits and pieces of the truth, twist them, and present them in a more positive light. You know deep inside that you're not giving an accurate answer. You know that you're not really communicating the truth.

Are you willing to shut down your need for immediate gratification in order to wait for your dream to come true?

Do you want your dreams to come true? If you're a truth manipulator, sooner or later people will learn not to trust you. You need the alliance of other people to help you reach your dreams and build your goals into success and reality. You don't want to be a truth manipulator. The Bible says "Thou shalt not . . . lie to one another" and the Hebrew definition of a lie is anything that is not the truth. So don't be a truth manipulator in your dealings with other people.

But there is another way of manipulating the truth, and it's even more dangerous. You can lie to yourself.

I have an excellent book by Robert Ringer titled *Million-Dollar Habits*. His first chapter is

"The Reality Habit." He says that the reason most people crash and burn when it comes to reaching their goals is very simple—they don't face reality.

Do you realize how much enormous energy you waste by denying the truth? Maybe you deny you weigh as much as you do. Maybe you tell yourself little lies in the morning about your appearance. Maybe you convince yourself that you're basically OK financially, but you're behind on your payments, and you're using MasterCard to pay VISA. You name it—you're not doing OK, and you're never going to do OK until you face the fact that you're not doing OK.

Lying to yourself about the reality of your present situation is a serious dream deflator.

4. *The firing of blame bullets.* You shoot blame bullets whenever you look for something or someone else whom you can blame for your failure.

There's a little story about a Little League game. The boy who played right field was having trouble. This little guy dropped three fly balls in a row. He blew it on three separate plays in the same inning. Finally the inning was over, and he came running in off the field. He took his glove, threw it down in total disgust, and said, "There is something really wrong out there. Nobody can catch a ball in that field!"

As the saying goes, "It's not whether you win or lose. It's how you place the blame!"

George Bernard Shaw once warned that you

have to be careful that you don't become so small and so shriveled in your personality that you become nothing but a feverish, selfish little clod of ailments and grievances, always complaining because the world will not devote itself to making you happy.

Do you know why your dreams won't come true if that's your attitude? It's very simple. It's because you're always wasting tremendous energy pouring the blame onto other people—shooting blame bullets—and hitting them where it hurts. For one thing, it takes energy away from your dream. For another thing, it alienates people—people you need to make your dream come true.

5. *Relationship poverty.* In many ways we live in a generation of isolation. People are so mobile; the average person moves five times or more in his or her adult lifetime. Most people don't live where they grew up. All this mobility generates a great deal of rootlessness. So many people today are lonely. So many are hungry for positive relationships.

Many people fail to achieve their dreams because they have isolated themselves from other people. We need good relationships to help us grow, to enable us to see ourselves honestly, and to give us encouragement.

Don't be so focused on yourself and your dream that you fail to work on your relationships. A lot of marriages fail for the simple reason that those involved in it don't work at it. As I've heard it said, most people put more time into planning a vacation than they do planning their married life together or even their finances. Relationship poverty will leave you empty, hungry for something only good relationships can fill. So while you reach your dream, make sure that at least part of your dream involves your wife, your husband, your children, your friends.

Let me go a step beyond that. You need to develop a relationship also with God. Through Jesus Christ, you need to involve God in your life and let him give you great dreams to strive after and to achieve for his glory.

When you fail in relationships, you'll fail in reaching your dream.

Don't be so focused on your own self that you fail to work on your relationships.

---

6. *Substance abuse.* Now, you think I'm talking about drug abuse or alcohol abuse, but I'm not, although those are certainly serious dream deflators. But I'm borrowing that term and using it emotionally, psychologically, and mentally. By my definition here, substance abuse means dissipating or throwing away your energy on what doesn't really matter.

Are you frazzled, worn out and fatigued,

wondering where all your energy went? The reason is that you've been working hard on things that don't count. You've been pumping away and not building your own future. Do you want to have financial energy? Then work for yourself, build for yourself, build your own business. The same thing is true in any area of your life.

Don't ever waste your energy and vitality on stuff that doesn't count. Always work for what matters. You don't want your life just to be filled with fluff, like a big, fat feather pillow. It may be comfortable, but it won't do anything for your life, and it'll make you soft.

This is the one area of life when you want to gain weight, mass, substance. You want to gain weight spiritually, mentally, emotionally, psychologically, financially. You don't want to be a lifelong lightweight.

Let me suggest something: Turn off your TV. It's just a big, fluffy pillow of nothing. Instead, read some great literature. Read the Bible. Fill your life with other people. Travel more. Gain weight by following great causes and giving yourself to a tremendous purpose in your life.

I want you to be financially free, and I want you to be a person of substance and weight in your life bank account, in your marriage, in your home, in your intellect, but most of all in your spiritual life. I want you to make a lot of money; I want you to be successful. So gain some weight in your bank account. But gain weight spiritually as well.

7. *Tension intolerance.* At MIT a major study was done on high achievers. It examined the common denominators of people of great success who reached their goals. The study discovered that one of the major reasons why winners win is because they have a tolerance of negative tension in their lives while they're building their dream.

You might think of it this way: Life is like living between two giant rubber bands. You're in the middle. On the left side is the status quo—where you are right now. On the right is your dream. Each of these is like a giant rubber band wrapped around your chest. Your current position is pulling you backward, and your dream is pulling you forward. You're caught in the middle, and it hurts. You have two choices: Stick with the pressure and win, or forget the pressure, lower your goal, and give up your dream. Two pressures—two choices.

It's like the bumper sticker that reads, "If all else fails, lower your goals." But that's not what the winner does. Writer Peter Senge says, "Escaping emotional tension is easy. The only price you have to pay is to abandon what you truly want, your goal or your dream." The pull hurts, but real winners are those who tolerate the pain long enough to reach their goal. One of the great characteristics of winners is that they can tolerate tension. That's why tension intolerance is a dream deflator, because while you're building for the dream, you hurt—with impatience, frustration, and rejection.

The MIT study found that the single greatest characteristic of a man or woman who succeeds in life is the ability to make it through the tension and through the negative feelings of frustration and impatience. Successful people develop a tolerance for tension, and they're able to reach their goals.

Learn the lesson I learned early in life and then again when I was recovering from a stroke. Don't let dream deflators let the air out of your dream.

Four
Build on the Right Foundation

*Strong lives are motivated by
dynamic purposes; lesser ones
exist on wishes and inclinations.
The most glowing successes are but
reflections of an inner fire.*

KENNETH HILDEBRAND

One thing I learned early in my career is the importance of building my dream on the right foundation. There are too many so-called successful people who are actually quite unhappy and miserable. I say so-called because I don't think these people are truly successful—they haven't built their dream on the right foundation.

There are five things that I think are very important in building your dream. I think these five things are necessities, not options, because they involve the foundation for your dream and your ultimate success. Without these five things, you won't achieve the goals toward your dream—you'll get sidetracked, or you'll run out of gas.

First, you have to build belief in yourself. How to Succeed in Business without Really Trying was a famous play on Broadway in 1961, based on a Pulitzer prize-winning novel of the same name. It's about a young man who is trying to maneuver his way up the corporate ladder. There's one scene in which the young hero goes into the executive washroom and walks up to the mirror. He's fighting a lot of negative pressure every day. People are pounding on him, criticizing him, trying to stop him from succeeding. They don't want him to go any further than he already has, but he wants to go all the way to the top.

Every morning he does the same thing. Every morning he performs this same ritual. He walks into the restroom, strides toward the mirror, and looks at the reflection in the glass. Then in a loud clear voice, disregarding the presence of any other men in the room, he says, "I believe in you!" Then he turns and walks out. Every morning.

If you don't think you're worth something, who else is going to think you're worth it?

He's reinforcing himself. If you don't think you're worth something, who else is going to think you're worth it? The Bible says you ought to love people as you love yourself. That means you have to believe in yourself first before you can love and believe in others. Gaze into the mirror, look yourself in the eye, and say, "I believe in you!" Reinforce yourself.

It may be that before you can truly respect yourself, you need to make some changes in your life. If there is anything in your life right now that violates your own personal sense and image of success, you need to stop that behavior right now and change it.

Gaze into the mirror, look yourself in the eye, and say, "I believe in you!"

One practical way of doing this is to make a list of the things you see in successful people that you admire. If your image of a successful person is some one who sits up straight at his desk, then teach yourself not to slouch. If your image of a successful person is some one who is always on time, then be on time yourself—make it a conscious habit. If your image of a successful person is that some one who avoids being a couch potato at night in front of the TV, then change your evening habits. If you don't, you'll find yourself trapped by those habits, and you won't ever respect yourself because you are constantly violating your own success image.

A second way of developing a healthy sense of self-respect is what I call "intelligent reconditioning." By this I don't mean brainwashing. I'm a Christian. I believe in the authority of God, a relationship with Jesus

Christ, the reality of the Word of God, and I don't believe in brainwashing. I don't believe in conditioning your mind in some weird way. But I'm talking about feeding your brain with the right input, nourishing yourself with the right mental diet. Maybe someday you'll have enough mental and emotional backbone that you'll be able to stand alone without any other support. But until that day comes, you need all the props you can get.

Fill your life with positive images and thoughts.

Could you tell from the nature of this book that I love collecting quotes from successful people? I have lots of great success quotes all over my home and office. I also collect things that are to me symbols of success. I walk into my office at my lake house, and do you know what I see? A giant eagle filling the whole ceiling of the room, in stained glass, with sharp, clear, brilliant light going through its wings, its eyes, its beak, and its powerful form. I have success symbols everywhere. These quotes and symbols remind me of basic truths about success and motivation—and they help me in my day-to-day life.

Fill your life with positive images and thoughts. Read books that help you generate ideas, that enable you to be more creative, and that give you greater motivation to pursue your dream.

A third way you build belief in yourself is by learning to surround yourself with the right people. There's a great verse in the Old Testament that says "Iron sharpens iron, so one man sharpens another." That means you need to be around sharp people if you want to be sharpened.

Earlier in my life, when I was building my career, I met a young man who had an interest in being part of my business. Frankly, I didn't trust him at first. He sounded too good to be true; he talked about his family's wealth, his contacts with famous people, and the fabulous house he lived in. But when I met his parents, they confirmed everything. They invited me to their home to meet some of their friends, and I suddenly found myself among the elite. Everyone at their home that night was independently wealthy.

It would have been easy for me to be intimidated. The group included some high-powered business people. But I remember that night thinking about my dream and saying to myself that these were the best people for me to be connected with. This could be a great foundation for my business. I forced myself to overcome my feelings of intimidation, and I spoke out and partcipated fully in the conversation. As it turned out, that night I won the respect of those influential business leaders, and I built many relationships with the top people in the area.

Sometimes building on the right people foundation means getting rid of the crumbling foundation that's already there. This is hard. You may have friends who have been close to you over the years, but you know they're not a good influence. Maybe their values aren't right, maybe they indulge in alcohol or drugs, or maybe they are always critical of people. It's hard to make these changes in your life, but it's important to do so. Perhaps you need to tell these people that you're trying to change your life and you need to avoid certain behaviors. Then see if they will make some changes themselves.

You need to be around sharp people if you want to be sharpened.

You need to manage your people environment. You have to learn a way to manage the negative around you, and you do that by managing the immediate people environment in your immediate situation.

Then there's a fourth way of developing belief in yourself—RSP. RSP is the Reverse Success Pyramid.

Normally, the structure of a pyramid has a

big base on the bottom, and it rises to a sharp apex at the top. In pursuing your dream, you have to reverse the pyramid because you don't have many successes to start with. It's tough at first. You build your dream—your great success—on the foundation of small successes. You get the pyramid started with a small success. And this is how you build belief in yourself. At first, you may not be so self-confident, and certainly you can't imagine being sure enough of yourself to achieve your whole dream, but you can have enough belief in yourself to achieve a small success. And with that small success your belief in yourself will grow, and you'll achieve something a little greater.

Let me ask you a question. Isn't it true that you have spent much of your life listening to your own failures? You've listened to them. They've been your teachers. Professor Failure has lectured your brain. Every day your mind goes to class and reviews all your failures from days and months before.

Well, don't you think it's now time that you learned from your successes? Even if they're minor successes. Even if they're at the bottom of the reverse pyramid. You have to start somewhere. The key is to keep building and growing until you get up to the top of your dream. Stop listening to your failures, begin listening to your successes, and build a healthy belief in yourself.

Second, you have to make sure you have a clean dream.

A clean dream is a dream that isn't mixed with something God condemns. You want a dream that helps people, honors God, and is morally sound.

Jesus said, "If you love me, you will keep my commandments." In all of my sucess, I have built on the belief that God's moral law—the Ten Commandments—are very much in effect today. God's laws of honesty, sexual morality, marriage commitment, and fair, loving relationships are the foundation of any *real* success.

Business has a bad reputation today because of the scandals of a few. Yet I work with fellow business owners who are themselves millionaires, who have developed profitable enterprises, and who have not violated the law of the Bible.

I am convinced that God gives special protection and blessing to those who build their lives *his* way. It is tempting to cheat as a shortcut, but the price is both too high and completely unnecessary. I would rather lose all I possess than to disobey the God of the Bible. But the great truth is I can build extraordinary success based on what he teaches in his Word.

My favorite book on success is actually in the Bible. It is the book of Proverbs in the Old Testament. I encourage you to read it and build your success on a solid foundation.

Someone once said, "Too many people climb

the ladder of success only to find out that it's leaning against the wrong wall." You don't want your dream built on the wrong things. If it is, you'll be in for a great disappointment later on.

Third, you need dream energy.

The MIT study that I mentioned before talks about the power of the dream gap—that's the gap between the dream and where you are right now. The study determined that great dreamers and great achievers take frustration and negative energy and turn them into positive energy. They use that frustration as fuel to make them work harder.

Stop listening to your failures, begin listening to your successes, and build a healthy belief in yourself.

The person with the losing attitude wallows in the negative frustration and emotions of failure. But the winner—the achiever—wants the dream so badly that he takes the frustration and negative energy and reroutes them in a positive direction. That becomes fuel—energy. It helps him overcome the dream gap and reach his goals.

The fourth thing you need is dream determination.

Another interesting thing the MIT study

discovered was that people who consistently succeeded were people who focused on their dream to the exclusion of everything else. Now this doesn't mean they forgot about their family or God and got their priorities out of whack. It simply means they were able to keep their focus clear, their eyes on the target, and they were able to keep out the clutter of false goals and peripheral issues.

Mr. Innamorya, the founder and president of the Kyocera Corporation, a firm that makes advanced ceramics for medicine and computer technology, was once asked, "What will it take to become a great success, to reach your goal?" He replied, "You will reach your goal when your passion and desire become so strong as to rise out of your body like steam." That is dream determination.

Someone once said, "Some men succeed because they are destined to, but most men succeed because they are determined to."

Fifth, you need to pay the price.

Paul Stern, the former CEO of Unysis, one of the largest computer giants of the world, said, "There's only one way to get where you want to go: that's to make up your mind where you're going and then go without excuses and without exceptions."

That advice works for everything from a diet to a business. Why do you fail at a diet? Because you allow yourself to offer up excuses and exceptions. "I'll stay on my diet unless I'm having a bad day." And suddenly every other day is a bad day. "I'll build my business just as long as everything else is in place." But it's never in place. You know why? Because you have to put it in place. It doesn't just happen. You have to know where you're going, and then you have to go there.

My coauthor, Ron Ball, uses a clever technique. He calls it A-B-GO. That means right now you are at point A, and you want to get to point B. Decide how to get there and go. A-B-GO.

What does this mean? It means you have to know where you are—point A. You have to know point B—specifying your target, a specific goal of your dream plan. And then you just have to get up and go. If you want point B—if you want financial security, if you want freedom and dignity, if you want to stand up on your feet again—you just get up and go. A-B-GO.

And whenever you get stuck or lazy or frustrated, you're going to whisper to yourself: A (that's going to remind you where you are), B (that's going to remind you where you're going), and GO (that's going to remind you what you have to do to get there).

It's simple but effective. Try it!

Five
Keep Your Momentum

*The road to success is marked by
many tempting parking places.*

ANONYMOUS

Success is the progressive realization of a worthwhile dream.

Have you ever gone to a baseball game and watched the kids in the crowd? It's great to see the dreams in their little eyes. You watch their hero worship of Roger Clemens and Ryne Sandberg and others on the field, and you feel their deep desire to become major league baseball players someday.

Recently I heard an interview with a rookie ballplayer, just up from the minors. He was very young and green and wide-eyed, and he talked about how incredible it was to be playing side-by-side with the great players of the game. And he mentioned that not so many years before he had been just a little kid collecting baseball cards of his baseball heroes. Now he was playing with them in huge baseball stadiums.

I listened to this young rookie talk, and I was reminded of this simple truth: Success is the progressive realization of a worthwhile dream. Success always starts with a dream that seems impossible, but when that dream is pursued and worked at, over time it gradually comes true.

Success is the progressive realization of a worthwhile dream.

I once met a garbage man who taught me an important lesson. He was intelligent—he had gone to college—but job opportunities were limited for him. He figured he had a lot to overcome, being black, so after college he decided to buy an old truck. It cost him forty-eight dollars a month. He found his first customer for four dollars a week, and he began to pick up garbage for a living. He became committed to his garbage business. He owned just the one truck, and he dated in that truck and went to church in that truck, even though it was junk.

This man and I were talking recently, and he said to me, "You know, last year I made $360,000 as a garbage man."

You see, this man had a dream. Maybe to some of us it's an unconventional dream—collecting garbage—but it was his dream nonetheless. Now my friend has seven men who work for him. But his dream didn't happen overnight. He worked hard the first years, doing the work himself, and then he gradually hired people to help him as his business expanded. Now he's a successful businessman, but only after working hard and taking one step at a time.

Sometimes it seems like we're working hard and nothing is happening. Success seems to elude us month after month, year after year. It's seems like we'll never get ahead. We keep working toward our dream, but we get discouraged and frustrated.

The hardest thing to do in pursuing your dream is to get it rolling from a standing stop.

Do you remember growing up? Do you remember when at a certain age you realized suddenly that some of your friends were members of the opposite sex? It was like overnight something changed. No longer was this the same person you played with in the sandbox or rode bicycles with. Suddenly he or she was different, changed.

Of course, nothing really happened overnight. Physical and psychological changes were occurring all along, but there came a day when those changes were suddenly realized, so it seemed like an overnight change.

I think this is often true also of the dreams that we pursue in our life. We may feel as if we aren't getting anywhere—we're working hard and getting discouraged—but if we are patient and if we persevere, there often is an "Aha!" experience that comes over us suddenly. It then seems like a sudden change, but in fact it has been a change long in the making—because of our hard work and effort.

Success takes time. It also takes effort and perseverance. Once you get your dream going, you have to maintain its momentum. You can't afford to stop along the way. The hardest thing to do in pursuing your dream is to get it rolling from a standing stop. You want to have to do that only once—the first time!

I have some suggestions to help you maintain your dream, to assist you in keeping your momentum. Some of these things will come easily to you; others will be more difficult. But in my personal experience I have found all of them to be timely tips toward maintaining my dreams and keeping my momentum.

1. *Learn from the best.* American industrialist Henry J. Kaiser once said, "I make progress by having people around who are smarter than I am—and listening to them. And I assume that everyone is smarter about something than I am."

The hardest thing for many people to learn is the art of seeking advice. We always think we can do something on our own. Instead, identify those people around you who are experts in an area, and humble yourself enough to seek their advice. Learn from those who have performed successfully and know what they're talking about.

2. *Strive for excellence, not perfection.* I believe that pursuing perfection is a waste of time. Perfectionism focuses on getting the details right. Excellence involves pursuing your dream by achieving your goals. Perfectionism takes extraordinary effort and extraordinary time to make sure trivial matters are exactly right. That's a "tempting parking place on the road to success," and it's a waste of time. Instead, maintain your momentum by striving for excellence—the progressive realization of your goals.

3. *Touch your dream every day.* Is your dream to own a Cadillac? Go to the Cadillac dealership every day. If it has to be after the dealership has closed, fine. Look at the car of your dreams. Is your dream to be financially independent? Look at your balance sheet and imagine zeroes in the liabilities column. Is your dream to build a house on a certain plot of land? Then visit that land every day. Kneel down and touch your dream. Visualize your house on that land.

The parking place that many people stop in after they have motored down the road toward their dream is the parking place of forgetfulness.

That is, they've forgotten the image of their dream. The inner fire has burned low, and people lose track of what they're after. They need to spend more time touching their dream so they won't forget and so the inner fire never burns out.

4. *Turn rejections into resources.* Every time somebody rejects you—your plan, your dreams—turn those negatives into positives. Consider the question of whether that person has a dream to pursue. Maybe not. At least you're pursuing a goal. Visualize yourself being in a superior position to that person in the future. Consider why that person was so critical— perhaps it is because he or she is envious and lacks self-confidence. Don't let negative comments sidetrack you from your dream. Turn rejections into resources.

5. *Work harder than anyone else.* The story is told of Fritz Kreisler, an accomplished American violinist, and a concert at which he performed. Backstage after the concert, a fan commented to Kreisler, "I'd give my life to play as you do!" Kreisler replied, "Madam, I did."

Don't let negative comments sidetrack you from your dream. Turn rejections into resources.

Thomas Edison is quoted as saying,

"Opportunity is missed by most people because it is dressed in overalls and looks like work."

In my book *A Millionaire's Common Sense Approach to Wealth* I wrote about the work principle. In fact, it's not so much a principle as just a plain fact. I wrote that "there is no truth that you must learn more urgently than the truth that success comes from hard work. It is all a matter of having a dream, and then work, work, work. Every person who has ever built anything significant has done so with labor—with the fuel and capital of hard work."

There is no truth that you must learn more urgently: Success comes from hard work.

---

6. *Get your priorities straight.* I believe that one's priorities should be God first, country second, family third, work/career last. You may arrange things differently, but I would urge you to make sure that your work and career don't take priority over the place of God and family in your life. I've seen too many marriages fall apart because someone pursued his dream at the expense of his family and his God.

7. *Give God the credit.* I'm always amused by the story about Horace Greeley and a United States congressman. The congressman said to Greeley, "I am a self-made man." Greeley

replied, "That, sir, relieves the Almighty of a great responsibility."

Too often when we're pursuing our dream we let our early successes go to our head, and we try to take the credit ourselves. When that happens, we invariably go on to make a mess of things. We get sidetracked in an empty parking lot.

I've always been open about my personal commitment to Jesus Christ. He's changed my life. I'm devotedly in love with him. I know that sounds strange to some people, but, believe me, he's real. I think the greatest secret of success is to know Jesus Christ personally.

God says in the Bible, "Let the Lord be magnified who takes pleasure in the prosperity of his servant." The Bible presents a balance of personal success and honor to God. That balance secures your proserity. If you honor God, he will bless you. If you don't, you will ultimately fail. When you try to achieve success on your own, it's not only wrong, it's dangerous!

Let me share with you a statistic that may surprise you. It comes from *Fortune* magazine (April 28, 1986). The magazine did a study of every CEO of the Fortune 500 companies. *Fortune* asked them, "Where did you get the values, the morals, and the beliefs to build your financial success?" Ninety-one percent of the CEOs said, "I've built my success on principles of success I learned in church."

These CEOs know the real source of truth.

That's why I don't apologize for making Jesus Christ a priority in my life. He's the one who got me here.

You need to give God credit in your life for the success you experience. The Bible says in the book of Psalms, "I will bless the Lord and not forget the glorious things he does for me." We should never forget the goodness of God—how he enables us to reach our dreams.

Consider these seven tips to help you maintain your dream. Don't let yourself get sidetracked and parked somewhere on a road off the main highway to your dream.

Dexter Yager and wife, Birdie, with actor George Kennedy.

Dr. Norman Vincent Peale and his wife, Ruth, with Dexter and Birdie.

Bob Hope with Dexter and Birdie.

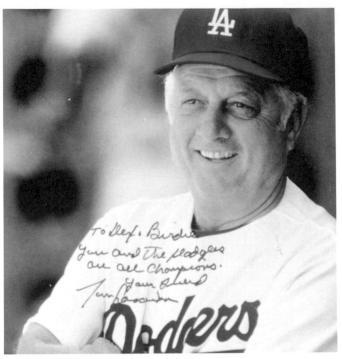

A personalized photo from Tommy LaSorda following a private business meeting in Hawaii.

Dexter with legendary entertainer Carl Perkins.

Actress Donna Mills during a charity event.

Actor William Shatner with Birdie and Dexter.

To Birdie and Dexter Yager
With best wishes, *Geo Bush*

Dexter and Birdie with President George Bush at a businessmen's dinner.

With entertainer Ronnie Milsap at his office and studios in Nashville.

Dexter and Birdie with Dr. Joyce Brothers.

Dexter, Birdie, and actress Debbie Reynolds in Las Vegas.

To Dexter Yager
With best wishes.
Ronald Reagan

With President Ronald Reagan at the White House.

Dexter and Birdie with Louise Mandrell.

Following a charity dinner, Henry Mancini with Birdie and Dexter.

Dexter, Birdie, and President Gerald Ford at a business associates' private reception.

Dexter and Birdie with Art Linkletter.

Dexter, Birdie, and comedian Tom Smothers in Las Vegas following a performance.

Paul Harvey and Dexter at the Charlotte airport in the early-mid 1970s, following a distributor rally.

Six
Develop Big-League Thinking

The intelligent person is not only open to new ideas—he looks for them.

ANONYMOUS

Too many people have big-league dreams and little-league ideas. I challenge everyone in pursuit of a dream to develop big-league thinking. One person I've challenged to grow in this area is my coauthor, Ron Ball. He tells an interesting story about the first time he was exposed to big-league thinking and a lesson he learned that has helped him at the top of his career:

"When I was a kid, I was introduced to the president of our local bank. He was a kind man, and he was especially gracious and generous to children. When I met him, he told me to call him by his first name. I thought that was pretty neat. Thereafter, when we would see other on the street, he would stop and talk with me.

"On one occasion, he told me his personal story and about the birth of his dream. I've never forgotten it.

"When he was a young man, his dream was to buy a grocery store. This was in an isolated, remote pocket of Kentucky. He had grown up there. He went to a local bank to borrow the money to make the purchase, but the bank turned him down flat. He was so infuriated by the rejection that he vowed to himself, *Someday, I will own this bank.* He walked out that day without his loan, but several years later he owned the bank."

The story that Ron tells shows big-league thinking. He dared to set for himself a remarkable goal, and he went out and achieved it. He had great gumption and guts. Big-league thinking is just that—the guts to set for yourself big-league goals and the gumption to achieve them.

Big-league thinking is the kind of thing that you know when you see it. It's a quality that's hard to define but is nonetheless very real. You can see this in sports. If you know fine basketball players such as, say, Michael Jordan and Magic Johnson, you can see in them something that sets them apart. They aren't simply good players; they are great players. And they are more than players playing a game—they are masters of the court, of strategy, of sportsmanship. You can see them control a game as it's played because they are thinking at a higher level than anyone else. That is big-league thinking.

Ron Ball tells of other big-league thinkers he has encountered:

"I remember when my wife, Amy, and I

encountered big-league thinking when we first arrived in Atlanta in the late 1970s. I had gone there to go to graduate school. We were in a car accident. I was driving a new top-of-the-line Ford, and a Cadillac ran into me, knocking me into a Mercedes. (It was a classy accident!) Amy and I were jarred and shaken, and there was much body damage to the cars involved. However, one of the insurance companies didn't want to pay on behalf of its client.

"I went to the pastor of the church where I was working and told him we needed legal help. I didn't know whom to turn to. He said, "I want you to go to a friend of mine. He is a corporate attorney and a Christian." I felt good about doing business with a fellow Christian, but I didn't realize at the time that this man was one of the most famous attorneys in the southeastern United States, a man whose clients included Coca-Cola, among other corporations.

"So Amy and I arrived at his office at the appointed time. Here I was, fresh out of school, and I knew very little. We walked into the elevator and immediately realized we were climbing to a new level of style and accomplishment. The elevator itself was thick with plush appointments, coated in brass, and trimmed in genuine leather. It was just incredible. We exited the elevator and walked into this attorney's office. It dripped of wealth. The attorney extended his hand to us and was most gracious and kind. He treated us with utmost courtesy. Amy and I sat there, and we realized we were in the big leagues."

Of course, big-league thinking isn't just the trappings of wealth. But it is true that big-league thinkers often are wealthy, precisely because their thinking has taken them there.

You need to be a big-league thinker, a big-league person, and you certainly want to develop a big-league business.

I want to give you something right now that I've shared in some of my seminars, something I'm very excited about—Four Steps to Big-League Thinking. Believe me, these steps will pull you into a higher level of success and achievement.

You need to expand your thinking, and here's how you do it:

1. Change your "ceiling image." Your ceiling image is your personal vision of how far you can go. It's your ceiling—the highest point you think you can achieve.

When I personally train business leaders, I try to get them to change their image of themselves. Here's what I do: I ask each person how he sees himself. I note the images each one uses to describe this—maybe he sees himself as a property owner, or a driver of a Mercedes, or a holder of public office, and so on. Then I say, "I know you can see that property, that car, that political office—you can touch your dream—but do you *see yourself as the person who owns that car, has that property, and holds that office?"*

You see, true success isn't a matter of acquiring great wealth or property or power. True success is the process of becoming the person who can achieve those things, the person who can handle those acquisitions. This means that for people to achieve their goals, they need to adjust their image of themselves—their ceiling image—and to strive to become the person who can achieve those goals.

Often it is in this area of self-image where the battle is won or lost.

Do you understand the concept? This is why many people who win the lottery are not successful people. They suddenly acquire wealth that far exceeds their ceiling image of themselves. They have, in a sense, been given success, but they have never become the kind of person who can handle it or manage it. This is why so many lottery winners have squandered their winnings five or ten years later.

Often it is in this area of self-image where the battle is won or lost.

There was a consultant named Alan Cox. Cox was hired by a manager named Tim. Tim asked, "Why can't I go further in my business? Why is it that I only go so far and then I just stop? Why can't I just punch through and go higher in my company?" Cox interviewed Tim, examined his procedures and patterns of business, and finally came to a conclusion. He said, "Tim, your problem is that you see yourself as second in command. That's your personal image of who you are, and until you drop that image, you'll always be second in command. You think of yourself as being 60 or 70 percent a leader. Until you see yourself as being 100 percent a leader, you'll never be first."

Until you see yourself as being 100 percent a leader, you'll never be first.

That's what I mean by your ceiling image. It is where you see yourself going. Some of you right now can see yourselves making another $10,000 a year, paying off your car, or getting a bigger home. That seems like a lot to you. But that's also a limit, your ceiling. That's as far as you can go.

I always ask God to help me live without ceilings. They don't exist for me. I never imagine, *Well, I've come this far, but look out, there's the ceiling—I've almost hit it.*

Ron Ball said he once counseled a young business leader and his wife. They were growing a strong business. He was a great guy, but he confessed to serious struggles in his marriage. He said, "I grew up with a negative relationship with my father. My father is very critical and domineering. We have always had a tense relationship. I determined I was not going to be like him, I was going to be different. And I started my business and I'm building, but something frightening is happening to me. I am now in my early thirties, I have children of my own, and I am beginning to realize with horror that I am becoming like my father. Can you tell me what causes this pattern?"

Ron began to explain to him this whole concept of mental images of ourselves and the ceilings we see in our lives. Ron suggested that this man's father had imprinted a certain image onto his own son.

Here's the way it works: As a boy grows up, he watches his dad. He wants to be like him, follow his footsteps, emulate the man of the house. But something happens at twelve years of age or so—he begins to develop a desire to differentiate himself from his father, he wants to become independent and establish his own individual identity. If his father has been negative and domineering and controlling, then this begins the battleground of the adolescent years. The boy is in a constant fight for identity, and this carries him into his twenties. Then in his thirties, the need for independence weakens—he is independent with his own

81

career and family. Then, *bang!*—he is at a moment of choice—an emotional psychological crossroad. At this point, because his desire for independence has weakened, because he has been independent all these years and doesn't have to fight as hard anymore, he makes a decision to keep striving for independence or to allow himself to naturally evolve into an image of his father.

If he becomes more like his dad, this might be good if the father is a great dad. But if the father is critical and harsh, the son faces an internal conflict: He is becoming more like the father he doesn't like.

Ron Ball went on to tell him that he had to make a choice. To allow himself to be limited by his father-figure ceiling image of himself or to expand his self-image to becoming something more and greater.

Let me tell you something. Some of you have your own self-image so wrapped up in your parents' estimate of you that you have not been able to rise above that. You need to respect your parents and get along with them, of course, but you must realize that you're adults and you don't have to be bound by the negative imprinting that they poured into your life, if you grew up in that kind of a situation. If you grew up with a great mom and dad—wonderful, praise the Lord. But if you didn't, you need to realize that this ceiling you keep bumping up against is stopping you from further success.

That ceiling may have been constructed by your parents. Maybe they didn't mean to—they loved you and maybe didn't intend it to happen—but the ceiling is constructed and you keep hitting it. So you must change your ceiling image.

You must learn to see yourself as a professional. A professional doesn't work nine to five. A professional does what the professional needs to do to make the professional's business work. That may mean working from six in the morning to ten at night. See yourself as a professional. Your work isn't a hobby but a business. See yourself at a higher level in your business. See yourself as a greater individual than what you think you are. See yourself beyond the ceiling that has held you down so long. See yourself in the big leagues.

2. Learn to communicate accurate information. One pattern of poor thinking that I see in many people is the failure to communicate true, accurate information. Many people have the tendency to gloss over the truth about their own situation when they seek advice from others. This, of course, often yields advice that isn't exactly on target.

Ron tells a crazy, true story that he and his wife, Amy, refer to as "the story of the boxes." One year they traveled to Europe. They were in London, about to board a flight to Paris. They had acquired a fair amount of baggage, and Ron asked the travel agent what the luggage limit was. He was informed that on the train trip they were scheduled to take from Paris to Brussels they would be allowed only one bag per person. To meet this restriction, Ron arranged to have their laundry boxed up and mailed back to the States by UPS.

The boxes were supposed to be waiting in Cincinnati when they returned from their trip. But Ron and Amy returned to Cincinnati only to discover that their boxes were actually sitting in Newark, New Jersey. Ron arranged to have the boxes shipped from Newark, but was informed by FAX that he needed to fill out forms and pay one hundred dollars to clear Customs. As it turned out, there were other mix-ups and more expenses, and ultimately it took four weeks and four hundred dollars for Ron and Amy to get their laundry back.

Here's the punchline. When Ron and Amy took that train ride from Paris to Brussels, they discovered that in fact there was no luggage restriction after all. One person had miscommunicated a simple fact, and had inadvertently caused a series of mishaps that caused Ron and Amy much inconvenience and four hundred dollars.

Not all failures of fact turn into such crazy situations. But, you know, it's interesting how often when something in a business or enterprise goes wrong, it's because some simple fact was miscommunicated along the way.

If you don't work with accurate information, you're in trouble. If you don't communicate accurate information, you'll get misleading advice and feedback. Tell the truth. Learn the crucial nature of accurate information. This is an important part of the proper thought process that's necessary for you to achieve your dream.

3. *Practice freedom speech.* I don't mean freedom of speech. I mean freedom speech. You need to learn the difference between *can't* and *won't. Can't* is the language of weakness. *Won't* is the language of decision. You say, "I can't go out tonight. I can't have a meeting. I can't follow up on this person. I can't get my checks in on time. I can't balance my checkbook in my business account." Do you hear the whine in your voice when you say that? If you say, "I won't do it," then you are taking the responsibility. It's a decision you are making. You are taking control.

If you say, "I can be financially independent; I can be free," you are making your success dependent on something outside yourself. If you say, "I will be independent; I will succeed," then you are making your success dependent on yourself, on what you will do. There is a world of difference. With freedom speech, you are speaking decisively.

This is more than just positive thinking. It is a breath of fresh air in your life. Just think—wouldn't it be a great relief, if you didn't want to do something in your business, just to be strong enough to say you won't do it? Not that you *can't*, but that you *won't*.

Make decisiveness a matter of personal pride. Whenever there's a decision to be made, you should say, "There's a decision here, and I'm going to make it." If you have trouble making decisions, let me urge you to do what industrial psychologists tell people in corporate management—start with small, little decisions. Build from there into making bigger decisions.

Remember that you're driving the car. There may be potholes, mixed signals, and slick surfaces on the road of your life, but there must never be any question as to who is driving the car. You are. Learn to avoid saying *can* and *can't;* train yourself to say *will* and *won't.*

4. *Develop a mind-set of responsible action.* A major corporate study found that the three biggest reasons for personal failure in business are poor attitude, fear of risk, and inadequate preparation. All three of these reasons are caused by wrongheaded thinking.

Poor attitudes usually occur when something goes wrong. The attitude might be one of looking for a scapegoat—firing blame bullets. It's been said that a man can fail many times, but he isn't a failure until he begins to blame someone else. Or maybe the attitude is one of self-pity—feeling sorry for himself. Either way, it's an irresponsible mind-set.

Fear of risk is another sign of bad thinking. Risk is necessary to success, and real achievers learn to take risks and to allow themselves to make mistakes. A successful man is usually an average man who took a chance.

Inadequate preparation is usually a sign of pride. Sometimes we think we're too good to put in the time and effort to prepare. This is immature thinking and a roadblock to real success.

These three prevalent causes of business failure are indications of a wrong mind-set. You need to develop a mind-set of responsible action: Take personal responsibility for failures, don't be afraid to take calculated risks, prepare thoroughly and do your homework.

Let me share with you a story. In the early stages of World War II, Franklin Roosevelt was desperately trying to rally the United States to support Great Britain in the fight against Adolf Hitler. Roosevelt was opposed by an organization called America First, which believed in a concept known as "Fortress America"—that we are protected by two giant oceans and should not dabble in the affairs of Europe. America First was an isolationist group and believed America had no business in the affairs of Europe.

Roosevelt believed that if America remained isolated and England fell, Hitler would aim his guns at the United States next. Roosevelt tried to rally America, while the America First organization fought him bitterly every step. Despite this opposition, Roosevelt was really concerned about the influence of just one man—renowned aviator Charles Lindberg, the most popular hero of his generation in America.

On September 11, 1941, America First scheduled a giant rally to mobilize support against Roosevelt. They were going to broadcast this rally all over America by radio. Charles Lindberg was the speaker. When they arrived at the hall in Pittsburgh, they received shocking news. The President was going to make an unscheduled speech that night. Because it was a speech by the President, every other speech was preempted. America First went ahead with its rally, but listened to Roosevelt's speech first, after which Lindberg delivered his rebuttal.

So that night Franklin Roosevelt broadcast what many historians believe was the greatest speech of his career. He talked about the courage of England, the violence of the attacks of the Nazis, the menace of Hitler, the grandeur of the British resistance, and the need to stand against Nazi terror. At the rally, the America First people became quiet as they listened to the radio broadcast. When the speech ended, Lindberg gave his prepared speech, urging people to disregard what the President said. But in his heart, he knew the battle for the hearts and minds of America was lost. Roosevelt had won.

Of course, history has proven Lindberg wrong and Roosevelt right.

After the event had ended, the senator who

had organized the rally talked privately with Lindberg. He said, "Charles, you shouldn't feel bad. We just got knocked out by the champ."

They knew that Roosevelt was a true leader and that he had gained the respect of the American people because of the quality of his thought and convictions.

I want you to see yourself like Roosevelt, a big-league thinker, a man with a quality mind-set and clear convictions. If you do, you can avoid some serious potholes of failure and be well along the road toward your dream.

Seven
Make Yourself Worthy

Try not to become a man of success, but rather try to become a man of value.

ALBERT EINSTEIN

Early in my life I learned that truly successful people are those who are at ease with themselves, comfortable in their relationships, and consistent in their personal values.

Let me put it another way. Many people will never achieve their dreams because they don't feel worthy of their dreams. A person who is ungracious with other people may achieve some small measure of success through his sheer determination, but ultimately he will fail because his dreams require the cooperation of other people. He won't succeed for long if he has to twist arms to get there. His is a bigger dream than he is a man.

A person who seeks success as a leader of a company, must be a person who is secure in his own life, at ease with his past relationships and comfortable in his present relationships. One who constantly wrestles with childhood traumas and the baggage of unresolved relationships will not succeed for long. His dream is bigger than he is.

It's important to make ourselves worthy of our dreams. H. G. Wells said, "Success is to be measured not by wealth, power, or fame, but by the ratio between what a man is and what he might be." You want to make what you are the same thing as what you might become. By changing to be the person you see in your dream, you'll help make your dream come true.

Let me suggest some ways in which you might make yourself worthy of your dream.

1. *Escape the temperament trap.* This is when you identify yourself as having a certain personality that seems to be fixed in cement. Let me tell you—if your personality is fixed in cement, so will your progress, your journey toward your dream. Probably the clearest sign of failure in a person's life is when he or she says, "I can't help it. It's the way I am. I was born this way."

Even though you were born with a certain personality style or blend or type, you can still change. Yes, you'll always have your essential personality type, the certain mix of faults and charms that are you. But you can learn, grow, and change. If you're too conservative, you can strive to be more adventurous. If you tend to be self-centered, you can work at attending to the needs of people around you. If you're shy, you can make efforts to be more aggressive. If you're a do-it-yourself type, you can learn how to include other people on a team. If you swing from emotion to emotion, you can strive to maintain some emotional balance in your life.

You can change. Your personality is not set in cement. Escape the temperament trap. Don't use the knowledge of your temperament as an excuse to stay the way you are. Make yourself worthy of your dream by changing the things in your personality that need improvement.

2. Learn to act contrary to your personality. Not always, but sometimes, it's good for you to battle your natural personality trait and act in an uncharacteristic way. Not only does it keep you from being too predictable, but it's a positive discipline in your life.

Let's take the fine art of negotiation as an example. Some people are just not very good negotiators. This doesn't have to be the negotiation of a major business deal—let's consider the purchase of a car. Many people don't negotiate well in these situations because they want people to like them. It's a character strength because they are friendly and outgoing, but in negotiating a deal it becomes a weakness. Any car salesperson will sniff out that personality trait and use it to his advantage.

What you need to do in this situation is simply force yourself, this one time, to act without too much emotion. There are many techniques to try. One is the technique of substitution. Pretend that you're buying a car for someone else, someone close to you, someone on a fixed income. Make yourself believe that you are representing the needs of this other person. So it's important to get a good deal, maybe under a specific price or monthly payment. Now the salesperson is not the only human being in the negotiation. Your natural people-pleasing trait can now act on behalf of this imaginary person whom you represent. You can afford to be tougher in the negotiation.

Whatever technique you use, it's valuable sometimes to work at acting contrary to your natural personality. Doing this gives you experience you will need later on, perhaps at a time when the stakes are higher. It stretches your character. It will make you more worthy of your dream.

3. Make friends with your childhood. Too many people are in a battle with their past life. Too many people are, as adults, still in conflict with their parents. Too many people are still wounded by past relationships.

If you have ghosts from the past, they will haunt your dreams in the future. Whatever your past consists of, you have to make friends with it. You cannot carry your past like a dead weight around your neck.

This is something God can help you with. I believe God is the greatest personality reconstructor in the world. I know people who have endured tragedy and trauma in their early lives. I've heard it said by psychologists who have counseled them, "They're going to be warped for life because of that negative experience in their past." And I have seen God rescue these people and transform their lives in ways that are truly unbelievable, miraculous. God can change you, forgive you, and bring healing for your emotions.

Dr. David Seamands has written great books on the subject of dealing with childhood traumas and healing damaged emotions. He talks about terrible experiences people had when they were growing up and how God would bring healing and help to key areas harmed in the past.

Make friends with your childhood.

4. *Develop "stand-back-ability."* If you want to maximize your personality, you need to develop stand-back-ability. This, quite simply, is the ability to stand back and look at yourself objectively. See yourself achieving your dream.

Are you the kind of person you would want to do business with? Do you have the personality you would feel good being around? If you were employed by yourself, would you enjoy you as a boss? Do you have the physical appearance that you, as an objective observer, would be attracted to? How do you look? How are your clothes? How are your fingernails? Do you have bad breath? Do you smell? Are you answering your mail on time? Are you speaking in a polite, courteous way with others? Are you getting the job done?

Perhaps this seems trivial, but in fact it can be terribly revealing and ultimately helpful. If you have stand-back-ability, you can more easily figure out if you are worthy of your dream.

Stand back and see yourself for who you actually are.

5. *Develop the art of social intelligence.* What I mean by social intelligence is the ability to get along with people in a happy, healthy, productive way. Social intelligence is much the same as what some refer to as "social graces," but with a few twists.

For one thing, social intelligence involves growing a strong political antenna. Pay attention to the way somebody says something. Develop an instinct for observing the way somebody answers a particular question. Examine the way a person deals with other people. Hear the hesitation in that man's voice; read the doubt in that woman's eyes. If you'll develop a good political antenna, you'll be sensitive to intangible things. You'll be a step ahead of the game.

Second, never intentionally embarrass anyone. Maybe it seems strange to you that I would even mention this, but, you know, there are many people on the road to success who have never learned this simple aspect of social intelligence. Using embarrassment to help yourself get ahead is a boomerang—it will invariably come back and cut your head off.

Remember, you need people to help you achieve your dream.

Third, use good manners. You have to realize that you have an opportunity to relate and interact with all kinds of people. The use of good manners is the oil that makes the machinery of life run smooth. There's a great section in the Bible (Galatians 5) that speaks of the characteristics, or fruits, of Spirit-filled living for a committed Christian. One of them is kindness. Kindness is love in action. It is how you show love to other people. I'm talking about good manners. Many people think, correctly, that success involves becoming a classy person. Many people think, incorrectly, that being a person of class means just driving a new BMW or sporting a large diamond ring. Real class means treating other people with consistent respect and kindness. Treat people with common decency, and you'll be amazed at the problems in your life that you will eliminate and the good will that you'll create which will help you achieve your dream.

Fourth, learn the art of asking questions. There are always difficult social situations, hostile audiences, and argumentative people. Successful people are great targets, and lots of people love to take potshots at them. One social intelligence technique for disarming hostility is to ask questions. This turns the arrows in the other direction. It also has the effect of getting the other person talking about himself, which is probably his favorite subject. If you're ever in doubt about how to pursue a conversation, particularly if there is antagonism, ask questions. Ask people about their homes, their dreams, their children. Ask questions that deal with what they care about. People love to talk about themselves.

Fifth, watch your language. I don't necessarily mean profane or vulgar talk, although certainly that has no place in your life (is such language consistent with your dream?). I'm referring to other kinds of speech turnoffs that you may be blind to. How do you refer to ethnic groups, to minorities, to women? Is your vocabulary offensive to these people? Do you tend to tell off-color jokes that embarrass people? Again, you need stand-back-ability. Find someone to observe you for a day or so and give you a report. Often we are blind to our own speech patterns.

Sixth, don't win battles—solve problems. That should be your approach with other people. Don't go in to win a battle—because if you do win the battle and lose the relationship, you've really lost the war. Winning battles is not why you have a business; that's not why you have a marriage. Many people fight to win battles because they have intense feelings of inferiority. They fight all the time. Part of the art of social intelligence is to remember that you're not in this to win battles; you're in this to solve problems.

Seventh, be positive with people. You must at all times be positive in your relationships and approaches with other people. Sure, sometimes you need to release negative tension by spouting off to someone, but make sure that someone is a person close to you who understands you and who can handle your outbursts. (Also, do make sure your outbursts aren't too frequent.) Otherwise, be positive with people. Why? Because people function more productively if they feel important and if they feel you care about them. Again, remember that you need people to help you achieve your dream. Treat them as being worthy of your dream, just as you are.

Make yourself worthy of your dream. Escape the temperament trap and be willing to change. Sometimes act contrary to your personality and stretch your character. Make friends with your childhood, and chase away the ghosts of the past. Develop stand-back-ability, a way of seeing yourself objectively. Learn the art of social intelligence, the simple graces of dealing with people.

This is how you make yourself a big enough person to fit the dream you strive to achieve.

Eight
Prevent Your Dream from Getting the Best of You

Pride goes before destruction and haughtiness before a fall.

PROVERBS 16:18

One of the most difficult lessons I've had to learn in life is something I find I have to learn over and over again. I learned it at the bottom, in the middle, and I keep relearning it at the top. It's a hard lesson because it has to do with our natural human tendency to let our success go to our head.

I'm talking about an overinflated ego. You have to prevent your dream from getting the best of you.

Recently a very successful businessman was talking about the future of business in our country. He said, "I believe the decade of the nineties is going to be the biggest, the greatest, the best that our business has ever seen. But we have one problem. The one thing that can derail our people and get them off the track of true success is pride. The one thing that can protect us is a strong dose of true humility."

I believe he's right on target.

Now anyone who knows me knows that I'm not much of a sports fan. But I am a fan of success, and sports has many lessons to teach regarding success that can be of help to business people.

It was fascinating to me to hear about the Chicago Bulls basketball team, which recently marched through the playoffs with a singleness of purpose and great focus. I understand that this was a team that won more than sixty games in the regular season. They came in first in their division, and then by defeating the Detroit Pistons, climbed into the championship series with the Los Angeles Lakers.

I am told that conventional sports wisdom holds that when a team gets to the finals the very first time, it very rarely wins the series; it takes a second attempt the next year. Do you know why? Because the first time a team gets to the finals, it goes to their heads. It's just like it often happens in business. The players see their great success; they lose their hunger to win. Then, when they lose the championship, they realize how close they came to winning it all, and they regret the loss. The next year, if they get to the finals, they concentrate harder. Their hunger is there, and they frequently win the series the second time around.

That's what made the Chicago Bulls remarkable. It was their first time in the championship series. They were playing the five-time champion Los Angeles Lakers. Youth versus experience. Many people expected the Lakers to win it all and for the Bulls to become satisfied and complacent and full of themselves, to lose the hunger for the ultimate win.

But somehow the Bulls stayed focused. Even when they went up three games to one on the Lakers' home floor, they refused to ease up, to start celebrating before the final game. You could see it in the press interviews—they were subdued and focused. They refused to let their success go to their head. And of course they won the fifth game and the championship.

Incidentally, maybe you were moved to see on TV the Bulls' locker-room scene after the final game. As soon as all the players were together in the locker room, they huddled together, and before any celebration began, they recited the Lord's Prayer. It said a lot about how they had their priorities in the right order.

We have to adopt the same mind-set about the success we achieve in life. We have to stay focused and realize that our dream hasn't yet been fully achieved. We have to tame our natural tendency to become puffed up and egotistical about our money, our success, and our status.

I'd like to share with you nine things that I have learned about preventing my dream from getting the best of me. These are the ingredients of basic humility, the cure for an overinflated ego.

1. Reject recognition resentment. You know the situation. You resent it when somebody else gets recognition and you don't. That's an indication that there is a raw sensitivity in your heart. You're easily offended, always watching, always testing the atmosphere and seeing if you are getting the recognition you deserve. Your antenna is always extended, picking up the signals: Am I getting the proper attention? Was I overlooked in that area? And you know when somebody else gets recognition that you think you ought to have, your resentment surges up like a volcano about to erupt.

Recognition resentment becomes a barrier to true success, and it's an indication of an overinflated ego and a lack of self-confidence.

That's the first characteristic of an overinflated ego. It's destructive in two ways. First, any kind of resentment eats away at your insides and begins to make you bitter. Second, it prevents you from learning from the experience. So, why did someone else get recognized? Why were you overlooked? Now, I'm not saying you don't need recognition—you do. Everyone needs encouragement. One of the great things about business is you can earn recognition and reward for what you do, and it's legitimate praise—you've worked hard and earned it. But if your ego gets so dependent on that recognition, and if you develop resentment when others get the glory, you're in for a fall. As the adage goes, "Every time you turn green with envy, you're ripe for trouble."

2. *Stifle the swagger.* This is the body language of arrogance. I'm sure you've seen it in others. You can tell by the way certain people walk and carry themselves. It's not the walk of confidence, it's a swagger, the walk of an overinflated ego.

Ron Ball told me of a time when he was in New York City. He saw a couple of professional male models walk into the hotel. Of course, they were in great shape, had a light tan, and were perfectly groomed. But you know, they kind of made him feel sick. It was because of the way they carried themselves. It was the swagger, the air of self-importance that they conveyed, even without speaking a word.

You need to ask the people around you—your spouse, your friends—if they detect the swagger in you. You need to watch this, because when you begin to swagger, your character begins to stagger. And when your character weakens, you're in for failure.

3. *Avoid the tendency of thinking you know everything there is to know.* When you make a deliberate choice to shut off your learning,

you're asking for trouble.

The story is told of the time that Sam Walton, of Walmart, and Jack Shewmaker, the president of Walmart, were visiting a competitor's store. This was a common practice of theirs: they reviewed their competition constantly. This particular store was an absolute mess. Shewmaker was walking around the aisles thinking, *Sam is not going to learn anything today. This place is awful. We're so much better in our stores.* The aisles were cluttered, the shelves were messy, and the service was terrible, but out of all of that chaos, Sam Walton stopped suddenly and said, "Jack, look at that. Look at that!" And he found on a single shelf in the middle of an aisle one tiny thing, a marketing gimmick, that inspired him. He said, "Jack, that's great. Why aren't we doing that?"

When you make a deliberate choice to shut off your learning, you're asking for trouble.

You know what Sam Walton has? He has humility. That's why he's the sixth wealthiest man in the world. He's never lost his humility.

The problem is that most people don't put those things together—humility and wealth. But Sam Walton never said, "I've finally made it. I know more than my competitor." And because he's refused to take that attitude, he's atop the number one retail chain in the world.

Don't let your ability to learn get overwhelmed by your success. You have to develop a right attitude of humility to learn, or you'll never get to the top, let alone stay on top.

4. *Beware the times when you can't get enough of you.* Don't talk so much about yourself. The book of Proverbs 27:2 says, "Let another praise you and not your own lips." The person who toots his own horn the loudest is usually in the fog. Not only is self talk an unbecoming personal characteristic, it's often strategically the wrong thing to do.

You have to develop a right attitude of humility, or you'll never get to the top.

The story is told of a young woman who moved to North Carolina. Her major in college was advertising, and she had landed an internship with an agency for a short time. While she was there, a full-time job opened up, and she asked her supervisor if she could apply for the job. Her supervisor set up an interview with the personnel office.

After the interview, the young woman, excited and gushing, couldn't stop talking to other employees, telling everyone that she had been offered the job. She said, "They really seemed to like me. I guess I have the background they want. They said I was great, that I have a wonderful future. It's really exciting. And, you know, I was hoping to get $17,500, but they gave me $19,500. I can hardly believe it." She went on and on.

Later, the supervisor asked the young woman how it went. The young woman told her the same things, going on about the interview and the salary she had been offered. Then the supervisor, in icy words, replied, "They're giving you $19,500? That's about what I make. And I've been here two years."

Don't let your ability to learn get overwhelmed by your success. You have to develop a right attitude of humility to learn, or you'll never get to the top.

The next day the young woman was fired. She went to management and asked why she was fired. They said, "You offended too many people, talking about your salary. You made things difficult, talking so much."

She learned the hard way.

Make sure that when you hear someone singing your praises, that (a) it's not a solo, and

(b) it's not you doing the singing.

5. *Refrain from saying things about others privately that you wouldn't tell them face to face.* Probably all of us have been in situations where we've been with a person, smiling and encouraging them, but then after they left, we've taken them apart in front of others, criticizing them and showing disrespect.

Of course, the Bible says that if we have something against another person, we are to go to that person and in front of a witness talk to them about that problem. That's good advice. Running people down is bad business, whether you're a motorist or a gossiper.

You know, gossip is a two-edged sword. If you gossip about others, don't you think others are likely to gossip about you? And if others hear you talking behind people's backs, don't you think they're likely to stop trusting what you say to them face-to-face?

Make sure that when you hear someone singing your praises, that (a) it's not a solo, and (b) it's not you doing the singing.

Besides being a matter of poor character, it's bad business to be two-faced with people. This kind of thing starts at the top of an organization and trickles down through the ranks.

Eventually a leader sees himself in his employees; they become like a mirror. If you see signs of disrespect and gossip and two-facedness in your organization, clean up the act, and start with yourself.

Stop treating people with private disrespect. It's a sign of arrogance and smugness, and it comes when we've had a taste of success and think we're the best thing since sliced bread. One thing I always pray is that I will never treat people with disrespect. I may not agree with them, and I may have to be firm with them, but I will not talk negatively about people behind their backs.

I'd like to suggest that the tendency to discipline people publicly is something that comes out of a sense of inferiority, a feeling of being threatened.

---

6. *Don't tear down people publicly.* While private disrespect is the practice of tearing down people (criticizing and being verbally destructive) when they're not around, public disrespect occurs in front of a crowd. Some managers deal with problem employees this way, using the fear of public humiliation as a negative motivator,

but in fact this is generally counterproductive. (Let me say, however, that I believe there are times in formal training situations where criticism of a person's performance in front of a group is necessary. There are positive ways of doing this, and usually it has an ultimate constructive purpose.)

W. Steven Brown, in his book, *13 Fatal Errors Managers Make and How You Can Avoid Them,* tells about the three ways of motivating people: fear, rewards, and belief building. He writes about fear, "Historically, this has been the most common motivational approach. And it smacks of manipulation. The manager normally uses it in one of two ways—either threat or actual punishment. First, let's look at threat. 'Produce or lose your job.' 'Produce or be humilated in front of your peers.' 'Produce or suffer any other dire consequences.' More often than not, the threat takes the form of a loss of personal dignity or esteem within the organization. True, if an individual (or a group) wishes to keep the job or please you badly enough, you can frighten him into performing. But over the long haul (and that's a matter of just a few weeks), the use of threat or fear as a motivational tool results in withdrawal or hosility on the part of the one threatened. . . . A number of years ago, I went to a dinner at one of the most fashionable restaurants in Milwaukee. Shortly after ordering, my waiter informed me that they could not serve me. They had to close for the evening.

When I inquired why, he told me that a disgruntled employee had exchanged salt and sugar in the kitchen. The chef triggered the incident by dressing down a busboy in front of the entire staff. The exchange of condiments was the employee's act of retaliation before quitting."

As Brown indicates, public embarrassment almost never works. But beyond that, I'd like to suggest that the tendency to discipline people publicly is something that comes out of a sense of inferiority, a feeling of being threatened. It's borne out of insecurity.

Many times in the pursuit of our dream things don't quite go the way we want them to, and out of our sense of desperation, we call others on the carpet and dress them down publicly. We're letting our dream get the best of us, and we're making a big mistake.

Many times in the pursuit of our dream things don't quite go the way we want them to, and out of our sense of desperation, we call others on the carpet and dress them down publicly. We're letting our dream get the best of us, and we're making a big mistake.

7. *Avoid criticizing things you know nothing about.* I'm sure all of us can think of someone we know who makes a habit of criticizing everything in sight. It's often a clear indication of an overinflated ego, although sometimes it's not so much a big ego as a small ego that is overcompensating. Either way, it's not good.

Ron Ball was in a group once where some men were criticizing the way Billy Graham's crusades were done. They were acting rather arrogant and cocky. But one of the men remained rather quiet. He was a friend of Ron's, and Ron knew him also to be a personal friend of Billy Graham. Ron asked him in front of the group, "What do you think about these criticisms?" This man stood up and said nicely but firmly, "I understand the comments, but until you've accomplished what Mr. Graham has accomplished, you really have no right to criticize the way he does it."

Sometimes it's just a matter of the work that you've invested that leads you to resist reality.

Constructive criticism is a valid thing. But it's based on a body of knowledge that one has about a subject. When we criticize matters that are out of our realm of expertise, we're acting out of an overinflated ego, and we've let our dream and our taste of success get the best of us.

8. Reject reality resistance. You probably have your theories of the way the world works and the way your business operates. You act on those theories, and many times those theories are part of your dream. But sometimes when reality differs with your theories about how things should happen, you resist the truth. You become so infatuated with your theories that you refuse to admit to the reality that's in front of you.

Sometimes it's just a matter of the work that you've invested that leads you to resist reality. My coauthor, Ron Ball, relates a good example of this.

"I normally take about three months to put together a presentation. That includes reading, research, cross-referencing, and making sure I can answer any questions. For every hour of public presentation, I prepare about ten hours of material; I never know what kind of question I'll be asked. This is just the level of commitment I've made personally. I do my reading, research, and study, and then I pray and ask God to bless it.

"But the hardest thing for me to do in preparation is to let my wife, Amy, critique my presentation before I go public. She's a good evaluator, but I resist the process of being critiqued, even though I know it's best for me. My presentation is a whole lot better after she finishes with it—or rather after she butchers it—it's all a matter of opinion!

"Apparently I had gotten to a point where I had forgotten how much I needed my presentations to be critiqued, and sometimes even butchered. She was evaluating me, but I was really resisting her criticisms. She would point out something, and I would simply argue with her and maintain that it was OK as it was.

"Amy got to the point several years ago when she said, 'Ron, I quit. I'm never going to help you with another outline. I don't want to hear it until you get on the stage.' I argued with her and implored her to continue critiquing me. She said, 'No, you're such a baby about it. You just argue with me. Every time I tell you something that I think needs to be changed, you just say it's good like it is. You aren't listening to me anyway. It's a waste of time.'

But if you take seriously the laws of God and obey them, I believe God will reward you.

"It was then I realized that I had a bad case of reality resistance. Of course, I had usually worked for two or three months on my presentation, and it was hard for me to accept the idea of making changes. So, I resisted reality.

"You know what is amazing? I cannot think of one positive, constructive criticism that Amy has ever made of one of my outlines that wasn't helpful. You see, every time she tells me something needs to be changed, in my heart and soul I know she is right. I don't like it, but I know she's right."

Ron's story perfectly illustrates the point. When our work and our dream seem to differ from the reality that confronts us, we tend to turn off the truth, and we embrace our dream blindly.

9. Don't treat the laws of God lightly. I don't know why it is, but often when people get a taste of success, they get so big-headed that they think they can get away with sin. Whether it's adultery or cheating on income taxes or lying or being careless with money, whatever, it seems that a little dose of success yields wrongdoing. Again, when you let your dream get the best of you; you begin to think you're on top of the world. In fact you're not—God is.

You fool yourself into thinking the rules don't apply to you. The Bible says in Numbers 32:23, "You may be sure your sin will catch up with you." And Romans 6:23 says, "The wages of sin is death."

Why do I say these things in a book about success? I say them because I believe they are a part of a bigger picture of success, a part of a bigger picture of your life. If you treat the laws of God lightly, you will pay a horrendous price. But if you take seriously the laws of God and obey them, I believe God will reward you.

Nine
Sometimes You Have to Fight

We have met the enemy, and they are ours.

OLIVER HAZARD PERRY

One thing I learned when I was still at the bottom of my career was that there are some things worth fighting for.

I still remember a friend of mine who laughed—actually laughed out loud!—at my new network marketing business. Because of that experience, I determined to fight to make my dream a reality.

Today when I drive in and around Charlotte, I can see the hundreds of apartments my construction companies have erected; I can see the millions of dollars of lake property I'm developing; I can see the thousands of distributors who pack into coliseums and convention centers to hear me speak. And I think then of that man who laughed at my dream. I thank God I didn't listen to that guy. I decided to fight for my dream, and it paid off.

Now, when I talk about fighting, people jump to two false conclusions. First, they assume I'm talking about other people. You may have certain people whom you believe to be your enemies, and yes, unfortunately it is necessary in the business world to stand up against certain people who wish to sabotage your life, your family, and your dreams. However, here I'm not talking about other people. Actually, I believe that most of the time our real enemy isn't other people at all. It is us. Or rather, It is inside us.

> I believe that most of the time we don't need to be fighting other people and that instead we need to be concerned about what we are fighting for.

The second false assumption is that I'm talking about fighting against something. I think that when we are simply fighting against something, we've lost our true motivation. In the recent Persian Gulf War, it was interesting to me to learn about the complete demoralization of the Iraqi army. Some of this had to do with the superiority of the U.S. and Allied forces. But what some commentators pointed out was that as captured Iraqis were interviewed, while they thought they were fighting against the U.S. military, they didn't really know what they were fighting *for*. To most Iraqis, the occupation of Kuwait was meaningless; it was Saddam Hussein's objective, not theirs. They weren't fighting to protect their country; they were fighting against another army. Consequently their morale began to break down from the start.

As I said, I think that sometimes we have to fight. But I believe that most of the time we don't need to be fighting other people and that instead we need to be concerned about what we are fighting for.

Let me suggest three things that are worth fighting for. There may be more in your life; you may think of others. But these, I believe, are significant matters that deserve your attention and demand active resistance on your part if you expect to be successful in achieving your goals.

1. *You have to fight for the purity of your mind.* I am convinced that the greatest enemy of success is inside us. It's an impure mind. You know, I love the book of Proverbs in the Bible. Proverbs are little nuggets of commonsense wisdom that pack a wallop when you think about them for a while. One Proverb says, "A wise man is hungry for truth, while the mocker feeds on trash."

127

What we put into our mind has a lot to do with what comes out of our mind. What we watch on TV, the music we listen to, the movies we attend, the magazines we read, the language we use—all of it influences what we produce in our life. You know the computer acronynm—GIGO. It's "Garbage In, Garbage Out." The garbage we feed our minds will result in garbage coming out in our life.

One of the great plagues of our century is pornography. Many historians consider the fourteenth century, the century of the Black Death, which killed about a third of all people in Western Europe, to be the most devastating period in Western history. As terrible as that was, I believe that very possibly the twentieth century plague of pornography will turn out to be even more devastating. We haven't even begun to understand the extent of the devastation. If pornography is a problem you wrestle with, fight it now. Fight for the purity of your mind.

Edmond Burke, the great English commentator, observing the French Revolution, said that it was an interesting social experiment, but the one danger he feared undid the whole revolution was its abandonment of moral principles. He said it de-stabilized a whole economy, a whole country, and a whole people. That's exactly what we've experienced in this country—spiraling destabilization. We need a moral foundation.

The Bible says that if a nation will be obedient to God and his principles of moral living, then God promises to protect that nation so the people of that nation can pursue his principles of life. Every great society in western culture in the last 500 years has been built upon principles from the Bible.

There are five great concepts that have come out of those principles: private ownership of property, respect for the institution of marriage, protection of the future of the children of that society, honesty and fair play among its people, and honor, reverence, and respect for God as the foundation. Whenever a society has all five of those traits, that society has remained strong. That is historically proven.

In 1940, a list was published of the top seven discipline problems in American public schools:

1. Tattling.
2. Chewing gum.
3. Making noise.
4. Running in the halls.
5. Getting out of line.
6. Wearing inappropriate clothing.
7. Failure to throw paper in a wastebasket.

In 1980, the top ten discipline problems in America's public schools were listed:

1. Drug abuse.
2. Alcohol abuse.
3. Teenage pregnancy.
4. Suicide.
5. Rape.

6. Robbery.
7. Assault.
8. Arson.
9. Gang warfare.
10. Venereal disease.

The moral character of our nation starts with you and the things you allow into your mind. Perhaps your problem isn't pornography. Even so, our culture plants ideas and images in our mind at every opportunity. That's why you have to guard what you allow yourself to watch and listen to and read. Fight for the purity of your mind.

The moral character of our nation starts with you and the things you allow into your mind.

---

2. Fight for free enterprise in our country. Joseph Dodge, no connection to the car of the same name, went to Japan on September 1, 1949. Dodge determined to teach the post-World War II Japanese a lesson in American business. Their whole economy was devastated. Douglas MacArthur had prepared the way; then Joseph Dodge came onto the scene. His program was so successful that even today Japanese leaders talk about the Dodge system, the Dodge program, the Dodge line. What did Dodge teach them that was so phenomenal?

One historian says that Dodge's approach was basically an American-Calvinistic approach. Dodge believed in the principles of business in the Bible, particularly in the Old Testament—the old-fashioned work ethic. So he taught them how to be good businessmen, save money, be frugal, work hard, not complain, be tough. There were many biblical principles bound up in his teaching. Proverbs 13:4: "The lazy will starve but the diligent will be rewarded." Proverbs 14:23: "Work brings profit." Proverbs 20:11: "Even a child is known by his actions."

Dodge told the Japanese that they would be known all over the world by their actions, and he pounded into them that the way to win was not to complain, but to work, work, work and to fight for their system of free enterprise.

We all know the outcome. Forty-two years later, in 1991, Japan has one of the largest amounts of venture capital in the world. They have followed Dodge's philosophy completely. The remarkable thing is that Joseph Dodge was in Japan for only three months. Three months and he transformed the nation. Some say that the reason he was so successful was because the Japanese were so hungry—they were passionate about success. They had been destroyed, but they hadn't lost their will to fight. They were willing to sacrifice to see their dream of a new Japan come true again.

We live in an era when remarkable things are

happening worldwide. We see the tearing down of the Iron Curtain. MacDonald's is in Moscow. Free enterprise has overcome communism. But, you know, some of the greatest resistance to the free enterprise system lies right here in the United States. We have a government that constantly intrudes on private businesses. We have politicians who want to introduce socialistic "reforms" into law, ideas that have in many cases already failed in other countries.

We need to be diligent, to fight for the principles of free enterprise in this country.

> # You will never live your life beyond your wildest expectations until you first have some wild expectations.

Let me tell you about Albert Jackson Stevens, Jr. His two sons are both listed in the Forbes 400 of the wealthiest men in America. Albert Jackson Stevens, Jr., was not a wealthy man himself, but he passed on his philosophy to his two sons. He told them, "I want you to remember one thing. You're poor right now. But your poverty is nothing to be ashamed of and your poverty is nothing to be proud of. Your poverty is something to be gotten rid of as quickly as you can."

A free enterprise system rewards creative

thinking, initiative, and hard work. In our country, success is possible for anyone who wants to put in the effort. Poverty is nothing to be ashamed of; it's just something to get out of as quickly as possible.

Fight for the system that has made our country great and that makes it possible for you to reach your dream.

3. *Fight for your dream.* Print Ball, Ron's father and a very successful businessman, once said, "You will never live your life beyond your wildest expectations until you first have some wild expectations."

You have to learn to fight for your dream. One of my first books was titled *Don't Let Anybody Steal Your Dream.* There's power in that thought. In order to protect your dream, you have to fight, and you have to have a will to win. If all you have is a wish for something more, you will never win. You may wish that Exxon had not spilled millions of gallons of oil in Alaska. But if you're not willing to do something about it, your wishes are useless. You may wish that 1.5 million babies per year are not aborted in America, but you are useless unless you are willing to do something about it. You may wish there were not a serious drug problem in this country. But that will do you no good unless you are willing to do something about it. You may wish that you were financially free, that you have a thriving business, or that you were free of debt and your home was paid for. You may wish you could drive the car of your dreams and vacation where you please and build the future that you hope for. You may wish for all of that, but it will amount to nothing unless you do something about it. You have to fight for your dream.

Ron Ball once put it this way: "Until your wish is connected with your will, you won't. You have to fight for your dream."

Until your wish is connected with your will, you won't.

Eight months after Pearl Harbor, the Americans mounted the most important counteroffensive of World War II. It was important because it was their first major offensive of any kind. They had been battered and beaten and embarrassed, and finally they were pulling in all of their resources to strike back. Eight months later, the American forces landed a small contingent of Marines on a tiny island in the Solomon chain known as Guadalcanal. This island was vital. The U.S. had to win. So they landed this small group of Marines and tried to drop as many supplies as they thought necessary. The Marines quickly took the airfield the Japanese had partially constructed, and they finished it and renamed it Henderson Field. They thought maybe that was going to be the end of it, but the Japanese had massed for an enormous counterassault. For the next several days and weeks, huge, almost overpowering Japanese forces pounded that tiny island. For months the battle swirled around that small piece of land. Seven major naval engagements took place during this span of fighting, including the worst single defeat in the history of the United States Navy. These young Marines, who were told to hold that island at all costs, were mostly young men in their early twenties. As they dug their trenches, they were scared, and most were physically sick because tropical disease was rampant. It was a desperate situation. These young Marines were clinging to their bases, hoping for reinforcements. Eyewitness accounts of the battles speak of seasoned Japanese veterans attacking day after day and night after night, hurling themselves at these green, young Marines, barely more than boys. One of the eyewitnesses said that the worst part of the early stages of the conflict was when the Japanese veterans would crawl forward, just out of rifle range, and in broken English would yell brutal insults at these young men across the battlefield, battering their morale and tearing apart their self-confidence.

One day, one young Marine suddenly became a very angry man. He stood up in front of everybody and hurled insults right back at the enemy across the battlefield. One by one his buddies started screaming with him. "You pieces of garbage. You try to take this island, you just try." They had been totally fed up and had had enough.

The whole battle began to change. Slowly the tide turned. Six months the battle raged, until finally those Marines secured Guadalcanal and won the first major offensive of the war.

I believe the reason they won was because that young boy stood up—he had had enough. He had the will to fight back.

If you want to succeed, you have to have the will to win, and you have to be willing to fight. Fight for the purity of your mind. Fight for the system that makes your dream a reality. And then fight, desperately, for your dream.

Ten
Discover the Special Ingredient

God will provide.

GENESIS 22:8

When I was still in my twenties and far from money, I lived through a period of painful disappointment. I lost my job, and, unable to find a new job for months, I fought with fierce feelings of failure.

I would drive through Rome, New York, during the night and early morning for a solution to my plight. I spent many hours reviewing what had happened to me and how things had gone wrong. All my hard work and positive attitude had not prevented the layoff. I hadn't been fired, but the job simply was no longer there.

My wife and children depended on me. Now I could not provide what they needed.

We survived, of course, and I worked again, but that experience threw emotional power into my decision to be financially free—to build my own business. Great good came from a time of wrenching pain.

Later, disappointment hammered me again

when the new network marketing business I had begun suddenly faltered and failed. Within months of reaching my first major business goal, my business was gone. I had to push back discouragement and start again, starting all over with nothing.

The lessons I learned from that failure formed the foundation of all my later business success.

The stroke I experienced in my mid-forties jolted all of us. The outlook was poor. My speech would be slurred. My legs would never work again. Another stroke could easily finish me off.

The doctor's prognosis turned out to be worng. Today I make major speeches every week to thousands of business people. I learned to walk again. My health has improved dramatically.

Those three discouraging experiences in my life have three things in common. They all seemed to destroy me at first. They all were overcome. And, most important, they all contained a certain ingredient that rescued me in each case.

That special ingredient is the basis of my life, my happiness, and my success. Let's look at those experiences again.

During those long months in Rome, New York, when I had no income and little self-esteem, that special ingredient gave me peace and strength. It increased my courage. It provided hope. In the midnight hours, as I drove the deserted streets of the city, that special ingredient worked inside my life.

Then, when my new business failed, the special ingredient was there to pull me back. It worked again, providing me the information I lacked and the direction I craved.

And when the shock of my stroke faded, and I was left with the greatest physical challenge of my life, the special ingredient was there for me. It became my recipe for recovery.

That special ingredient in my life is not a secret. It is available to everyone. It is simply this: a personal relationship with Jesus Christ. I believe it was Christ who resued me in the dark days of Rome, New York, who helped me rebound from my business setback, and who enabled me to recover from my stroke.

I received Jesus Christ into my life when I was very young. The reality of this relationship in my life has never weakened. Christ is the fuel and force of my life today.

Maybe you're not the "religious type." Then I have something to say to you. Jesus Christ is not a system of religion. He is a living person who loves you. He can be your special ingredient for success as well. It's as simple as this: Turn your life and behavior over to his love and authority.

Jesus said, "I am the way, the truth, and the life. No one comes to the Father except by me."

He is the foundation of true success.

OTHER BOOKS
BY
DEXTER AND BIRDIE YAGER

Don't Let Anybody Steal Your Dream
Dexter Yager with Douglas Wead

This classic in the field of motivational writing has sold more than a million copies and is selling as well today as it did in 1978 when it was first published. Dexter Yager has influenced millions with his forthright honesty, compassion and desire to see others succeed. Here is a man who has "made it" in all the right ways, and who is willing to pour out the ideas that make for successful living.

Stock No. BK-10 Paperback

The Secret of Living Is Giving
Birdie Yager with Gloria Wead

Birdie Yager, wife of one of America's most famous and powerful businessmen, talks about:
- Marriage: How to make it work.
- Attitude: The way to popularity and self-esteem.
- Your Husband: How to make him rich!
- Children: When to say no, and when to say yes.
- Health and Beauty: They are result of our decisions, and are not automatic.
- Money: When it is bad; when it can be wonderful.
- Faith in God: Why you must deal with your guilt and inferiority, or self-destruct.

Stock No. BK-96 Paperback

143

Becoming Rich
Dexter Yager and Doug Wead

Inspirational and moving stories of some of the world's greatest people and the eleven principles behind their success. Includes Walt Disney, Albert Einstein, Martin Luther King, Andrew Carnegie, Adoph Ochs, Jackie Robinson, Thomas Edison, Helen Keller, Harry Truman, Coco Chanel, Winston Churchill, Arturo Toscanini, and Douglas MacArthur.
Stock No. BK-97 Paperback

Millionaire Mentality
Dexter Yager with Doug Wead

At last! A book on financial responsibility by one of America's financial wizards, Dexter Yager! Dexter gives freely of his remarkable business acumen, teaching you how to take inventory and plan for financial independence.

Here is a common sense, down-to-earth book about investments, shopping, credit and car buying, and budgeting time and money.

Included are anecdotes about other successful American business people—to give you ideas about where to go from here!

If you are serious about financial planning, this is the book for you!
Stock No. BK-206 Paperback:

A Millionaire's Common-Sense Approach to Wealth
Dexter Yager with Ron Ball

Financial principles on which to build your life and your dream. Based on Dexter Yager's own life-tested success secrets, this book provides valuable instruction and direction for those who are just beginning to get a vision for success. Learn common misconceptions people have about money and materialism; Disover the eleven reasons to be rich (some may surprise you!); read about the five keys to financial prosperity—the dream principle, work principle, perseverance principle, investment principle, and people principle; break down the budget barriers in your own life; and learn common sense perspectives on managing money. This book will help you turn your life around.
Stock No. BK-315 Paperback

The Business Handbook
Dexter Yager

The most comprehensive how-to-do-it manual ever offered!
A simple yet detailed guide that lets you chart your own path to success in Amway.

The Business Handbook brings you the best in proven techniques regardless of whether you want to earn just a little extra income or if you are interested in building a large successful organization.

Discover what MLM or Network Marketing (as revealed in Megatrends) really is and how it differs from Direct Marketing and Pyramiding. Awaken yourself to the proven advantages offered through the Amway phenomenon. Learn about:
- Winning
- Leadership
- Goalsetting
- Loyalty
- Dreambuilding

Discover the secret techniques used by many successful distributors who have become millionaires and are fulfilling their greatest dreams.

Stock No. BK-247 Paperback

Successful Family Ties: Developing Right Relationships for Lasting Success
Ron Ball with Dexter Yager

Right relationships with the people around you are fundamental to your success in life—emotionally, spiritually, and even in your work. This book will give you high-performance, practical guidelines for dealing with the many important issues that may be holding you back from experiencing success in your family relationships. You'll learn to recognize the signs of trouble and to take steps toward overcoming:
- ruptured relationships
- busy signals in communication
- sexual temptation
- stress
- negative people

And with principles founded on God-given, timeless truths you'll discover lasting success in all your challenges and be sure to have successful family ties.

Stock No. BK-310 Hardback

Mark of a Millionaire
Dexter Yager and Ron Ball

Character principles that will change your life. Develop the traits that are common to successful business people. From becoming a dreamer to being hard-working, from overcoming fears to seeking good counsel, from becoming a pioneer to establishing yourself as a person of integrity—these classic character principles are the foundation for success.

Stock No. BK-334 Paperback

Everything I Know at the Top
I Learned at the Bottom
Dexter Yager and Ron Ball

Personal stories and lessons from the life of Dexter Yager provide insights into the keys to success. Read about Dexter Yager's early boyhood experiences selling soda pop to construction workers; learn the important business principle he picked up from his early days selling cars. Out of these personal accounts from the life of a successful leader, you can learn valuable lessons for use in your career and your life.

Stock No. BK-351 Paperback

Available from your distributor, local bookstore, or write to:

Internet Services Corporation
P.O. Box 412080
Charlotte, NC 28241-8834
